RAND

China

Domestic Change and Foreign Policy

Michael D. Swaine
with Donald P. Henry

Prepared for the
Office of the Secretary of Defense

**National Defense
Research Institute**

This report documents one component of a multi-year effort to analyze the political-military, social, and economic dimensions of change across the Asia-Pacific region over the next 10–15 years, highlighting those changes that might prove potentially adverse to U.S. interests. The goal of the research is to delineate a set of indicators within the various dimensions—an indicator being an event, process, or development that portends possible changes with negative implications for core U.S. policy assumptions and regional security objectives.

The report was produced under the aegis of a project entitled *Reevaluating Asia: Regional Indicators and U.S. Policy.* Other reports in the project cover the following topics:

- Asia's Changing Security Environment: Sources of Adversity for U.S. Policy

- Change in Taiwan and Potential Adversity in the Strait

- Japan: Domestic Change and Foreign Policy.

This research was sponsored primarily by the Office of the Under Secretary of Defense for Policy. It was carried out under the auspices of the International Security and Defense Policy Center within RAND's National Defense Research Institute (NDRI), a federally funded research and development center sponsored by the Office of the Secretary of Defense, the Joint Staff, and the defense agencies. Supplemental funding was also provided by the RAND Center for Asia-Pacific Policy.

CONTENTS

FIGURES

TABLES

This report analyzes the implications of political-military, social, and economic developments within China for the evolution of Chinese foreign policy over the next 10–15 years, especially policy toward the Asia-Pacific region. The purpose of such analysis is to discern whether and in what manner the profound changes that have taken place within China since the late seventies could prove adverse to U.S. interests in Asia. The analysis thus treats domestic political-military, social, and economic trends and features as largely independent variables. Important external influences upon Chinese policy—for example, the actions of critical actors such as the United States and Japan—are discussed primarily within the context of such domestic factors.

This report concludes the following:

- Domestic changes over the next 10–15 years will almost certainly not produce a significantly more democratic and pro-Western Chinese regime; neither will they lead to the emergence of independent regional power centers or the complete breakdown of political rule in China.

- China's existing authoritarian government and foreign policy will likely continue for many years into the post–Deng Xiaoping period, the latter marked by overall caution and pragmatism, a recognition of the need for a placid regional environment to permit a continued emphasis on economic reform, and a balancing of both cooperation and competition with the West.

- Such policy continuity will nevertheless pose significant challenges to Asian security, deriving primarily from the regional anxieties produced by China's continued economic growth and military modernization; yet such challenges *should* prove manageable over the next 10–15 years.

- However, far more adverse Chinese external behavior could emerge during this period from existing Chinese domestic trends; the most serious of these will likely derive from various forms of military intervention in internal politics and foreign policy, resulting from problems in economic policy and the increasing influence of ultraconservative nationalistic sentiments.

- On balance, a *moderate* level of success in China's reforms is in the best interest of the United States and China; both significant setbacks in the reform effort leading to a severe downturn of the Chinese economy and sustained, very high rates of economic growth and increased central government revenues resulting from the resolution of major reform problems could result in serious domestic instability and adverse shifts in Chinese external behavior.

- Similarly, *moderate* annual increases in China's military budget are also in the U.S. interest, as opposed to either very high (10 percent or more) or very low (0–5 percent) increases; either of the latter could precipitate highly adverse shifts in Chinese domestic politics and foreign policy.

- Although not a primary focus of this study, the behavior of foreign countries, and especially the United States, could greatly alter the above assessments; in particular, strong, public U.S. pressures on China in a variety of areas could greatly increase the likelihood of strongly anti-Western conservative nationalists gaining control of the Chinese political system.

- To minimize the chances of the most adverse Chinese outcomes, the United States should, at a minimum:

  1. Strengthen and expand both official and unofficial contacts with Chinese civilian and especially military leaders

  2. Avoid vaguely defined or broadly punitive economic or diplomatic actions against China, insistent and direct de-

mands for democratic political change in China, or U.S. actions that could be viewed as attempts to take advantage of internal disarray

3. Encourage more extensive and durable economic links between China and the United States that promote moderate Chinese growth, and support more general measures that strengthen the overall importance of external economic relations to China's future growth and stability

4. Establish greater coordination and communication on China policy with regional allies and friends, especially Japan, South Korea, Australia, and key ASEAN countries

5. Maintain current U.S. military force levels in Japan and South Korea and clarify the division of labor between a power-projection-oriented United States and a primarily defensive-oriented Japanese military.

ACKNOWLEDGMENTS

This report has benefitted enormously from the labors of many individuals. Among RAND colleagues, I would like to thank Donald Henry for his assistance on Chapter Four. I owe a special debt of gratitude to my very talented and conscientious research assistant, Kirsten Speidel, who provided invaluable support throughout every stage of the project, from initial research to final editing and revision. Deborah Elms and Jessica Steele provided the graphics and charts and also assisted in proofing and checking the manuscript. My secretary, Barbara Wagner, pulled together the final version of the manuscript and provided all manner of logistical support. I am also grateful to Patricia Bedrosian and Michele Guemes of the RAND Publications Department for final editing and production.

The report was formally reviewed by David M. Lampton, President of the National Committee on U.S.–China Relations. The incorporation of Dr. Lampton's many insightful comments and suggestions served to greatly improve its overall quality. Valuable written reactions to early versions of the report were also provided by William Overholt of Bankers Trust (Hong Kong); Brigadier General Michael Byrnes of the U.S. Embassy, Beijing; and Bonnie Glaser, a Washington-based consultant on Asian security affairs.

Finally, the analysis of Chinese leadership trends, social attitudes, and foreign and security policy views benefitted greatly from discussions held in Beijing during 1993 and 1994 with several knowledgeable Chinese strategists and officials. These individuals requested that their names not be cited in this report.

ACRONYMS

ACFTU	All-China Federation of Trade Unions
ASEAN	Association of Southeast Asian Nations
CC	Central Committee
CCP	Chinese Communist Party
CITIC	China International Trust and Investment Corporation
CMC	Central Military Commission
CPPCC	Chinese People's Political Consultative Conference
FASLG	Foreign Affairs Small Leading Group
FDI	Foreign Direct Investment
GLD	General Logistics Department
GNP	Gross National Product
GPD	General Political Department
GSD	General Staff Department
IAEA	International Atomic Energy Agency
MoFA	Ministry of Foreign Affairs
NPC	National People's Congress
PAP	People's Armed Police
PLA	People's Liberation Army
PRC	People's Republic of China
R&D	Research and Development
SEZ	Special Economic Zone
U.N.	United Nations
VAT	Value-Added Tax

Chapter One

INTRODUCTION

Internal forces shape the tenor of China's foreign relations, often in decisive ways. At present, the linkages between domestic events and China's effect upon the Asian security environment in particular are arguably stronger than ever before, for several reasons. First, China's impending leadership succession and the more general transition to a new generation of Chinese civilian and military elites present major implications for China's future stability and regional policy. Second, China's opening to the outside world and the rapid marketization of its economy have increased the ability and desire of social groups to influence domestic and foreign policy issues. This process of dynamic social mobilization also creates the prospect of enormous internal unrest, with accompanying negative implications for the regional security environment. Third, China's booming economy, upon which the legitimacy and stability of the central government increasingly rest, relies on close economic, managerial, and technological connections to the outside world, especially to the United States and Asia. Finally, continued high economic growth rates and contacts with the outside world are essential to the success of China's military modernization effort, which stands at the center of its comprehensive strategy for coping with the post–Cold War security environment and will likely have major implications for Asia's future peace and stability.

These internal and external linkages suggest that developments in three domestic areas will exert an enormous influence over China's external stance over the long term and thus will provide possible indicators of adverse change, especially toward Asia:

- *In the political-military area:* the changing composition of the central and provincial civilian and military leaderships, the nature and extent of elite support for continued reform, and the open-door policy toward Asia and the West

- *In the social area:* evolving public attitudes and behavior toward political reform and the authority of the communist regime and divergent intellectual views of China's changing security environment

- *In the economic area:* the effect of continued reform and development on the changing pattern of economic capabilities and controls, external economic ties, and the military modernization effort.

The report begins by describing and analyzing, in three separate chapters, those domestic trends and features in each of the above areas that will most likely influence China's long-term external behavior. A fourth chapter discusses the major implications of the above trends for the primary features of China's future global and regional policy. This discussion includes an analysis of several types of adverse foreign policy stances that could emerge over the long term, each associated with various continuities or discontinuities in Chinese global and regional policy. One very positive type of policy stance—a highly cooperative China largely supportive of U.S. interests in Asia—is also analyzed. For each stance, the precipitating role of particular political-military, social, and economic trends and features is examined. This provides the basis for a preliminary listing of several possible indicators of each foreign policy stance. The fifth and final chapter contains a brief discussion of several possible implications that the above analysis presents for U.S. policy toward China and Asia in general.

Chapter Two

POLITICAL-MILITARY LEADERSHIP TRENDS

China remains a country governed by personalities, not laws or institutions. In the history of modern China, individual leaders such as Sun Yat-sen, Chiang Kai-shek, Mao Zedong, Zhou Enlai, and Deng Xiaoping have exerted an inordinately high level of influence over the course of events, especially in the foreign policy realm.

The role of the dominant leader could again prove decisive to China's future evolution, including its stance toward the Asia-Pacific region. However, although important, any attempt to identify a future Mao or Deng is fraught with enormous difficulties and could easily prove futile. Little reliable information exists on the internal workings of China's top elite to evaluate which leader or group of leaders will likely emerge to direct the country's future, especially over the long term. Instead, more systemic, structural trends relating to the changing composition and likely policy views of China's emerging generation of leaders, along with their relationship to key bureaucratic organizations such as the military, provide a far more reliable basis for understanding the future effect of leadership on China's political stability and policy direction. This chapter focuses primarily on such structural trends among two key leadership groups:

- Party-government leaders
- Military leaders.

PARTY-GOVERNMENT LEADERS

During the past fifteen years, a wholesale transformation has taken place in the composition, outlook, and regional orientation of China's political leadership, with major implications for long-term foreign policy outlook and behavior. The most basic features of this leadership transformation include:

- The civilianization and specialization of leading party and government figures, replacing the party-army political "generalists" of the past with development-oriented bureaucrats and technocrats

- The emergence of strong unifying forces among this new leadership, centering on a common pragmatic approach toward continued economic (but not political) reform and increasing general support for a state-centered form of patriotic nationalism

- The existence of several potential causes of leadership conflict over the medium and long term, including both latent policy divisions and narrower power rivalries

- A change in the provincial composition of the central party leadership and a relative shift in political and economic authority from the center to the periphery.

Civilianization and Specialization

Since the advent of the reform period, and especially following the Twelfth Party Congress of 1982, China has witnessed a major change in the training, career experiences, and regional backgrounds of political leadership at all levels. The founding generation of revolutionary leaders with extensive experience in both party and military areas has gradually been replaced by (a) better-educated, almost entirely civilian career *bureaucrats* and (b) well-trained, specialized *technocrats*. The former group currently dominates the leadership at both the central and local levels, consisting largely of senior party and government apparatchiki with practical administrative skills but little formal education in finance, engineering, or other sciences and virtually no direct military experience. The latter group is subordinate but growing in importance.[1] It includes an increasing number of civilian technocratic experts trained in finance, engineering, and industry management who provide essential advice on developmental issues. Together, these two leadership groups form an interdependent and younger "bureaucratic technocracy" that has served as both the beneficiary and the main bulwark of the Chinese reform effort for nearly fifteen years.[2]

Data presented in Tables 2.1 and 2.2 reflect the emergence of this new elite. The former shows a significant drop in the average age of party Central Committee members since the beginning of the reform period in the late seventies, and the latter indicates a remarkable increase in their level of education.[3] Other analyses of long-term leadership changes show an increase in urban political experiences and career patterns and an overall increase in the percentage of specialists, from 1.79 percent in the Ninth Central Committee to 20 percent in the Thirteenth Central Committee.[4]

The emergence of this new leadership coalition in China marks the end of nearly thirty years of political dominance by rural-oriented "generalist" leaders whose authority was based primarily on control

---

[1]Although a significant percentage (around 23 percent at the center and 37 percent at the provincial level) of Central Committee members and other elites are technocrats, a career in the party organs or the government system still contributes greatly to "claiming high" in the power hierarchy. See Xiaowei Zang, "The Fourteenth Central Committee of the CCP: Technocracy or Political Technocracy?" *Asian Survey*, Vol. 33, No. 8, August 1993, p. 792.

[2]Zang (1993), especially pp. 800–801. Zang states that the interdependent nature of this new leadership coalition derives from the fact that the bureaucrats rely on the technocrats for their expertise and advice, whereas the technocrats require the assistance of the bureaucrats to advance their positions within the government hierarchy. It should be noted, however, that a growing number of Chinese central and local leaders possess *both* bureaucratic and technocratic expertise.

[3]Zang points out that the current provincial leadership (defined as secretaries and deputy secretaries of the provincial, municipal, and autonomous region committees of the party) is even younger than the leadership at the center. Cadres aged 60 and above make up 57.14 percent of the Fourteenth Central Committee, whereas this age group constitutes only 18.47 percent of provincial leaders.

[4]Li Cheng and Lynn White, "The Thirteenth Central Committee of the Chinese Communist Party: From Mobilizers to Managers," *Asian Survey*, Vol. 28, No. 4, April 1988, p. 380.

Table 2.1

Overview of the CCs (Eighth to Fourteenth)

CC	Year	Female Rep. (%)	Minority Rep (%)	Avg. Age
8th	1956	4.0	5.2	56.4
9th	1969	7.6	4.6	59.0
10th	1973	10.2	5.6	62.0
11th	1977	6.9	5.7	64.6
12th	1982	5.2	8.0	62.0
13th	1987	5.7	11.2	55.2
14th	1992	7.5	10.3	56.3

SOURCES: Li and White (1988), pp. 371–399; *Lianhe Zaobao* (Singapore), October 20, 1992; and Zang (1993). © 1993 by The Regents of the University of California. Reprinted from *Asian Survey*, Vol. 33, No. 8, August 1993, pp. 794–795, by permission of the Regents.

Table 2.2

Percentage of College Educated Members Serving in the CCs

CC	Percentage
8th	44.3
9th	23.8
10th	NA
11th	25.7
12th	55.4
13th	73.3
14th	84.0

SOURCES: David Bachman, "The Fourteenth Congress of the Chinese Communist Party," *Asian Update,* The Asia Society, New York, November 1992, p. 3; and Li and White (1988). © 1988 by The Regents of the University of California. Reprinted from *Asian Survey*, Vol. 28, No. 4, April 1988, p. 379, by permission of the Regents.

of ideology and mass organizations and who enjoyed extensive links to the military.[5] This new leadership is clearly better suited to the

---

[5]See Li Cheng and David Bachman, "Localism, Elitism and Immobilism: Elite Formation and Social Change in Post-Mao China," *World Politics*, Vol. 42, No. 1, October 1989, pp. 64–94. The authors state that between 1982 and 1988, more than

formulation and implementation of complex economic reform policies than their predecessors. However, unlike their predecessors, almost all the members of China's emerging leadership lack both strong ties with military leaders and broad-based personal contacts that span party and state organs. Such serious political deficiencies could well hamper the ability of future leaders to wield effective power over the long term (more on this point below).

Greater Policy Consensus and Growing Support for State-Centered Nationalism

China's new civilian leadership is less divided over key domestic and foreign policy issues than its revolutionary predecessors. In the past, China's economic and social development was repeatedly disrupted by fierce internal political disputes between radical Maoists holding utopian or ideologically motivated views (usually hostile to the West) and more cautious and orthodox Marxist-Leninists. Since Mao Zedong's death in 1976 and the emergence of the reform movement under Deng Xiaoping in the late seventies, however, the views of the former group have been almost entirely repudiated and their major exponents purged while many of the most orthodox views of the latter group have been either discarded or significantly transformed. Such changes, combined with the strong support for higher levels of economic development found within the military and broad segments of society (discussed below), have created a strong and virtually irreversible consensus among China's leadership in favor of a strategy of pragmatic economic reform keyed to extended marketization and links with the outside. This policy consensus is reinforced by a strong belief among China's leadership in the critical importance of continued economic development to future social stability and regime legitimacy, emerging as a result of the erosion of confidence in the capabilities of the party apparatus and the disenchantment with party ideology that has taken place in China since the late sixties.[6]

550,000 better-educated young cadres came into leadership posts above the county level, whereas 2,870,000 senior cadres recruited during the pre-1949 struggle for power were retired under a program of leadership reform devised by Deng Xiaoping (p. 65).

[6]This process of regime delegitimization resulted partly from the inevitable process of routinization and bureaucratization that affects all revolutionary movements and

Although some members of this emerging leadership generation hold strong suspicions toward the West (and Japan), most recognize that China's economic reform strategy requires the maintenance of good relations with such countries, at least over the short to medium term.[7] However, support for economic reform and continued contacts with the West have not led to a similar level of leadership support for political liberalization. China's bureaucratic technocracy is fiercely protective of the power and prerogatives the reforms have provided it and is strongly committed to the notion that social instabilities caused by the transition from plan to market (e.g., unemployment, corruption, crime, and a general weakening of social discipline) can be kept in check only through continued firm authoritarian political controls. Hence, while a few political leaders may harbor some sympathies for limited democratization in China, most will permit a loosening of the political system only on the margins, to facilitate or maintain continued economic development.

In addition to a common emphasis on reform-led economic development and a general recognition of the continued need for a monolithic, authoritarian political order, China's emerging leadership is also increasingly supportive of a state-centered form of patriotic nationalism. This notion, intended to compensate for the all-too-evident weaknesses of socialist ideology and to rally popular support behind the communist regime and its policies, draws upon traditional attitudes that favor a well-ordered and hierarchical political structure, strong popular emotions regarding past injustices suffered at the hands of foreign powers, and deeply rooted desires for greater international status and respect. It also plays upon the growing sense of pride felt among ordinary Chinese citizens concerning China's recent economic and diplomatic accomplishments, discussed in greater detail in Chapter Three.

---

partly from the enormous upheavals and policy fluctuations that took place in China during the sixties, seventies, and early eighties, centered on the Cultural Revolution. See H. Lyman Miller, "The Post-Deng Leadership: Premature Reports of Demise?" *Washington Journal of Modern China*, Vol. 2, No. 2, Fall/Winter 1994, pp. 1–16, for a particularly persuasive argument on the level of policy consensus among China's successor leadership.

[7]Some may even be supportive of much greater levels of cooperation with the West, as discussed below.

This form of nationalism thus identifies "the nation" most closely with the Chinese state; moreover, it seeks to defend the vested interests of the current authoritarian political system, not to challenge it in the name of an enlightened "modern" or "liberal" nationalism, as was the case in earlier Chinese nationalist movements. It presents the image of an economically and militarily strong Chinese state capable of redressing past grievances, resisting current and future foreign intrusions, and wielding a high degree of influence in the international arena, at least on a par with other major powers.[8] Moreover, it is being promoted by China's political leadership through campaigns of "patriotic education" that emphasize the need to remember earlier sufferings at the hands of the West and Japan, prevent the loss of Chinese identity through foreign cultural and political intrusions, and accept the need for strong government controls over society, deemed essential to the creation of a wealthy and powerful country.[9] The overall importance attached to such nationalist views by China's bureauratic-technocratic leadership is reflected in the fact that patriotism now often stands ahead of collectivism and socialism in official statements defining the core ideas of the communist regime.[10]

---

[8]As Lucian Pye points out, this image of a state-centered nationalism, defined in terms of international power relations and reflecting the attributes and aspirations of a partisan group of political leaders, lacks the collective cultural ideals and shared inspirations and myths that can both nourish a positive public conscience and place limits on the behavior of the leadership. In other words, this form of nationalism is equated with blind patriotism, not with more inspiring cultural ideals and beliefs that reflect the abilities and successes of modern Chinese. See Lucian W. Pye, "How China's Nationalism Was Shanghaied," *The Australian Journal of Chinese Affairs*, No. 29, January 1993, pp. 107–133.

[9]A more hardline variant of this form of nationalism, generally associated with a school of thought labelled "neo-conservatism" by outside observers, places a particular stress upon the need to limit Western involvement in China and rely more on military—as opposed to primarily economic or diplomatic—instruments of foreign policy. This viewpoint, discussed in greater detail below, is especially prevalent among *some* members of the new generation of Chinese military leaders.

[10]For this point, and further details on the nature of China's growing nationalistic sentiments, see Wang Jisi, "Pragmatic Nationalism: China Seeks a New Role in World Affairs," *Oxford International Review*, Winter 1994.

Several Latent Policy-Based Sources of Leadership Strife

Although the political and ideological spectrum in China has narrowed enormously under the reforms and the incentives for leaders to cooperate have arguably increased, several policy issues could eventually produce a pattern of intensifying argument and even open conflict among them. First and foremost among these is policy toward the economy. Despite the above areas of consensus, significant latent differences exist among the emerging civilian leadership over the desired *pace* and *extent* of economic reform. At the core of these divisions is a debate between a politically dominant group of relatively cautious, socialist bureaucrats and a weaker yet rapidly rising group of more radical yet authoritarian reformers. The socialist bureaucrats (many of whom were trained in the former Soviet Union) place a primary emphasis on the maintenance of social stability and strong government control, especially at the central level. Hence, they generally oppose both the full-scale marketization of the economy and *any* movement toward political liberalization. Instead, members of this group favor a relatively slow, incremental pace of policy implementation, a continued strong role for the party, and the maintenance of planning controls over key sectors of the economy, such as heavy industry, energy, and transportation. Many supporters of this outlook also resist the dismantling of China's large number of inefficient state enterprises, mainly because they believe such actions would lead to social disorder. In the central elite, this group is made up largely of party and government apparatchiki, many from the more conservative yet reform-oriented east and northeast.[11]

The radical reformers support a more rapid pace of advance and a much greater reduction in government controls than the socialist bureaucrats do. While agreeing on the need for order and discipline through strong government, the radical reformers are more willing to run risks of inflation, limited social unrest, and ideological heresy to

---

[11]The extreme conservative end of this group includes an apparently small but vocal contingent of leaders supportive of expanding the socialist sector of the Chinese economy and greatly reducing the presence of foreigners. These views are influenced by the more rightwing or "neo-conservative" proponents of patriotic nationalism, mentioned above. In the civilian sphere, such individuals reportedly reside primarily within the heavy industrial ministries and the propaganda apparatus. This point was conveyed to the author during discussions with Chinese strategists in fall 1994. The presence of such views within the military is discussed below.

accelerate market-driven economic growth, arguing that ". . . rapid economic growth over the long term would help Chinese authorities deal more effectively with social and other dislocations stemming from economic and other changes."[12] Also, this group *might* contain a small minority of individuals supportive of limited government concessions toward a more genuinely open political system, in order to ensure continued popular support for rapid economic advance. Members of this group include both technocrats and bureaucrats, but are most often found among the former, and probably also receive significant support from younger leaders and entrepreneurs in the more dynamic and free-wheeling south. However, they apparently enjoy little influence among key central bureaucracies and the military.[13]

Neither of these groups should be considered a cohesive, self-conscious, or broadly based leadership faction per se. Each constitutes a diffuse, informal "alignment" of leaders with similar views in one particular policy area, yet with differing motives and perhaps an uncertain awareness of their common membership. Moreover, it is unclear whether the differences between these two alignments are severe enough to negate the above areas of agreement that exist between them. The ability (and willingness) of either group to contend with the other over the long term will almost certainly depend upon the type of future economic policy issues or problems confronted by the regime and, most importantly, the future capability of each broad grouping to acquire key "representatives" or champions at the very top of the leadership structure.

Several high-level party figures within the emerging civilian leadership coalition appear to be associated, to varying degrees, with these

---

[12]See Robert G. Sutter, Shirley Kan, and Kerry Dumbaugh, "China in Transition: Changing Conditions and Implications for U.S. Interests," *CRS Report for Congress*, Congressional Research Service, Library of Congress, Washington, D.C., December 20, 1993, p. 8. Also see William H. Overholt, *The Rise of China: How Economic Reform Is Creating a New Superpower*, Norton, New York, 1993, p. 99.

[13]The extreme "liberal" end of this group includes those few individuals within the emerging leadership who support the near complete dismantling of the state sector, a further devolution of economic authority to the localities, and a rapid push toward a market economy marked by private holdings in land and capital and the free flow of labor. Proponents of this extreme view are primarily found in *some* local and provincial governments.

two contrasting economic policy alignments, although their level of commitment to each viewpoint is difficult to gauge. Li Peng, currently State Council Premier, Politburo Standing Committee member, and reportedly Chairman of China's Foreign Affairs Small Leading Group (FASLG),[14] displays the most consistent support for the views of the conservative socialist bureaucrats. He has often stressed the need to maintain a viable state enterprise sector, for example, and generally takes a cautious approach to new reform initiatives. A second leading supporter of the conservative socialist bureaucrats is Vice Premier Zou Jiahua. This group also receives significant support from Jiang Zemin, CCP General Secretary, PRC President, and putative successor to Deng Xiaoping.[15] However, Jiang has been something of a "fence-straddler" in the past, also at times espousing elements of the radical reform agenda. Zhu Rongji, Politburo Standing Committee member, Bank of China President, and State Council Executive Vice Premier, is probably a more consistent supporter of radical reform, albeit of a variant that stresses a relatively high level of central control over the economy. Two other Politburo Standing Committee members, Qiao Shi and Tian Jiyun, also probably support at least some elements of the radical reform viewpoint.

On balance, the views of socialist bureaucrats probably exert greater influence within leading party and state organs at present, largely

---

[14] Reports have emerged in recent months that Li has lost his chairmanship of the FASLG to Jiang Zemin. This is highly unlikely, but if true, it would mark a significant loss of influence by Li within a critical policy arena.

[15] In addition to his position as top party and state leader, Jiang is also a Politburo Standing Committee member and chairman of the organ charged with direction of the military, the party Central Military Commission (CMC). He also heads several major leadership small groups that exercise executive power over key policy arenas in China such as the central financial and economic group, the Taiwan affairs group, and the political-legal affairs group. In addition, Jiang Zemin's personal secretary, Zeng Qinghong, heads the General Office of the Party Central Committee, which wields enormous formal and informal influence within leading party organs. This concentration of power gives Jiang considerable authority over personnel selection and decisionmaking across many policy arenas. See Wu Futang, "Jiang Zemin Holds Six Key Posts, and Ba Zhongtan Is Being Transferred to Beijing to Command China's Armed Police Forces," *Kuang Chiao Ching* (Hong Kong), No. 3, March 16, 1993, pp. 6–9, in *FBIS-CHI*, March 22, 1993, pp. 15–18. Also see Wei Li, *The Chinese Staff System*, Institute of East Asian Studies, Berkeley, 1994, p. 18.

because of the general support extended by Li Peng and, most recently, Jiang Zemin. However, in recent years, and especially since the Fourteenth Congress of the Communist Party, held in the fall of 1992, the political position of the radical reformers among the central civilian leadership has improved greatly, primarily as a result of the death or retirement of powerful conservative elders, the promotion to top central posts of additional supporters, and Deng's unequivocal public support for more rapid reform.[16] Yet the basic tension remains between the two leadership groups over the pace and extent of reform and could play a very important role in political maneuvering at both central and local leadership levels during the post-Deng period.[17]

Other important policy issues outside the economic arena might also serve to generate significant conflict among China's emerging civilian leadership, especially over the long term. These include the pace and extent of military modernization, China's future foreign and security policy stance, and the future handling of critical social and political events such as the Tiananmen incident of June 1989. Views on these critical issues almost certainly vary significantly within the emerging bureaucratic-technocratic leadership and could become more pronounced in the future, although the specific content of such differences is not as evident, and their implications for the top leadership as "easily" identifiable, as in the economic arena. These non-economic issues and their potential for generating leadership strife are more closely examined in subsequent chapters on military leadership and social/intellectual trends and in the concluding chapter on foreign and security policy.

---

[16]Further details on the strengthening of the radical reformers' position are contained in Sutter et al. (1993), pp. 8–9. Also see Michael D. Swaine, *The Military and Political Succession in China: Leadership, Institutions, Beliefs*, RAND, R-4254-AF, Santa Monica, 1992, pp. 193–195.

[17]A key issue that will likely emerge soon after Deng's passing will be whether leadership support for more critical (and difficult-to-implement) fiscal, legal, and price reforms can be sustained in his absence, especially if major economic problems such as inflation and declining government revenues intensify. See Chapter Four for further details.

Nonpolicy Sources of Leadership Strife

The above potential policy divisions within the emergent civilian leadership are complicated, at least over the short to medium term, by the existence of other more purely power-related factors directly connected to the leadership succession process. On the broadest level, the absence of any institutionalized and regularized process for wielding and transferring supreme political power in China creates a general climate of insecurity and distrust among the top leadership that could lead to an escalating—and prolonged—power struggle in the months and years following Deng Xiaoping's death.[18] Such a struggle might reinforce differences within one or more of the above-mentioned policy arenas and eventually threaten the stability of the communist regime.

The likelihood of such an expanding power struggle is increased by two specific features of the senior Chinese leadership: (1) the presence of a small number of generally unpopular top conservative party leaders closely associated with the Tiananmen repression, and (2) the existence of assorted "failed" aspirants to power who remain in the wings. The former group is currently represented by Premier Li Peng, mentioned above. Li was the initial "victor" in the leadership struggle of the Tiananmen period that resulted in the ouster from power of former Party General Secretary Zhao Ziyang, a strong proponent of radical reform. He thus became a highly unpopular symbol of violent repression and intolerance. Li Peng's political fortunes have declined considerably in recent years, however. Although respected for stabilizing the economy after the 1988–1989 inflation and restoring China's diplomatic prestige after the Tiananmen incident, Li continues to encounter strong opposition in the party and society and among many (especially younger) military officers. He also suffers from a heart condition and is expected to retire from his post as Premier after the completion of his current term. Moreover, he lost a critical political supporter with the death in April 1995 of his primary patron, Chen Yun. Nonetheless, Li Peng could still wield considerable power in a post–Deng Xiaoping setting,

---

[18]For further details on the systemic sources of leadership instability, especially as it relates to the succession process, see Michael D. Swaine, "Leadership Succession in China: Implications for Domestic and Regional Stability," paper prepared for the RAND-Sejong Project on East Asia's Potential for Instability and Crisis, February 1995.

particularly if allied to other influential figures, and might initiate (or become the object of) a destabilizing power play.

The leading members of the latter group include former People's Liberation Army (PLA) General and Political Department head Yang Baibing and his older half-brother, former PRC President and CMC First Vice Chairman Yang Shangkun. Both men, along with several of their supporters within the military, were removed from power at the Fourteenth Party Congress in the fall of 1992, reportedly for attempting to develop a factional network designed to control the post-Deng succession and overthrow Jiang Zemin, their major political opponent. Although currently off the political stage, the Yangs (or Yang Shangkun alone) could attempt a comeback in a post-Deng setting. As a member of the revolutionary generation, the elder Yang retains considerable prestige and extensive organizational contacts. Moreover, he is still respected in some leadership circles as a skillful party administrator and a leader of the reform effort in the mid-eighties, including military reform. His return to power would be especially likely if key Yang opponents among the retired military elders were absent from the political scene, and if the successor leadership became embroiled in a protracted struggle over policy.

A further complication is presented by the continued presence in the political wings of former party leader Zhao Ziyang. Zhao was a major proponent of radical reform, decentralization, and the open door in the eighties and a strong opponent of the use of military force during the Tiananmen incident. Hence, he could conceivably play an important political role in any post-Deng succession struggle as a lightning rod for various progressive (or purely ambitious) forces opposed to those conservative socialist bureaucrats, such as Li Peng and Jiang Zemin, who directly benefitted from the Tiananmen crackdown. After Deng's death, individuals allied at the central and local levels with both radical reformers and perhaps even political liberals might attempt to align with (or use) Zhao in an effort to force a reversal of verdicts on Tiananmen and thereby undermine the position of Li and Jiang.[19]

---

[19]Such an alliance might include both radical reformers at the center, such as Zhu Rongji, Hu Qili, Rui Xingwen, and Yan Mingfu, and local leaders most closely associated with greater provincial and regional independence, such as former Guangdong governor Ye Xuanping. To be successful, however, this alliance would almost certainly

Partly to prevent such scenarios (and generally to strengthen his claim to the succession), Jiang Zemin has made concerted efforts to improve his personal ties to China's military leadership since 1990, while also portraying himself as supportive of professional military interests. Key officers such as General Zhang Zhen, Vice Chairman of the Central Military Commission, and Defense Minister Chi Haotian are believed to be his strongest supporters within the military. There are also indications that Jiang is attempting to establish a base of support within the People's Armed Police (PAP), a key organ charged with the maintenance of domestic stability and a crucial buffer between society and the regular military. In 1993, Jiang named a supposed protégé, Ba Zhongtan, commander of the PAP.[20]

A final complicating factor is presented by the offspring of China's original revolutionary leadership, the so-called "princelings." Many of these individuals play an influential role in key economic and military-related bureaucracies. However, few are currently viewed as politically ambitious figures in search of greater party or state power. Instead, most are thoroughly dedicated to making money or, in some few instances, climbing the military hierarchy, but this situation could change rapidly after the passing of Deng and his elder associates. Many princelings could become targets of veiled—or open—attacks, as the excessively privileged (and often corrupt) sons and daughters of party and military elders. Such attacks could serve as a catalyst for broader opposition to the communist regime and thus precipitate or intensify conflict within the party elite and between state and society. Under such circumstances, several senior princelings could assume a more prominent political role, perhaps allying with one or more of the above elite groupings to decisively shift the balance of forces within the civilian successor leadership. Alternatively, they might disperse their presence across all major

---

need to obtain the support of current or former senior figures such as Qiao Shi and perhaps even Yang Shangkun. For a provocative discussion of such possibilities, see Robert Delfs, "Zhao Ziyang in the Shadows: Prospects for Party Liberals in the Succession Struggle After Deng Xiaoping," paper prepared for the Fifth Annual Staunton Hill Conference on the People's Liberation Army, June 17–19, 1994.

[20]For an exhaustive examination of Jiang's efforts to strengthen his hold over China's armed forces, see David Shambaugh, "China's Commander-in-Chief: Jiang Zemin and the PLA," paper prepared for the Sixth Annual AEI Conference on the People's Liberation Army, June 1995.

leadership groupings and thereby lessen such influence, while still aggravating general opposition to the regime.[21]

Shifting Provincial Representation and Greater Local Authority

The emergence of the above generation of civilian bureaucratic technocrats also signifies a shift in the geographical origins of central political leadership in China. During the fifties, sixties, and seventies, revolutionary cadres from south and central China provided the bulk of the party and state leadership. However, since the advent of the reforms, the coastal areas, especially the eastern provinces of Hebei, Jiangsu, Shandong, and Zhejiang, have increasingly provided the core of China's new civilian leadership. However, only a very small percentage of these central cadres originates from the economically dynamic south China region (see Table 2.3).[22]

Of even greater significance, the reforms have also resulted in a major devolution of authority from central party and government organs to provincial and subprovincial political leaders and enterprise managers, as well as the emergence of unofficial private and semiprivate business elites enjoying close links to local officials but also possessing independent control over economic resources. Overall, this trend has occurred as a natural consequence of the decentralization of economic decisionmaking authority and the dilution of central government controls that took place in the mid and late eighties, discussed in greater detail in Chapter Four. Such changes greatly increased local government influence at the provin-

---

[21]See the appendix for a listing of the leading princelings and their current positions. For a fascinating analysis of various princeling groupings within the party, state, and military systems, and within industry, see *An Eye on China,*, No. 10, Kim Eng Securities, Hong Kong, January 1995.

[22]Zang (1993), pp. 790–800. As indicated in Table 2.3, cadres in the Central Committee from the east coast total 35.99 percent, from the north/northeast coast 19.58 percent, and from the south coast only 2.65 percent; a disproportionately large number of provincial and municipal leaders are also from the east. However, several leaders from Guangdong province entered the Central Committee as alternate members at the Fourteenth Party Congress, which suggests that Beijing may be attempting to remedy the growing imbalance between economic and political power in China. Still, it is too early to tell if such an adjustment will be carried through.

Table 2.3

Geographical Distribution of Members of the Fourteenth CC

Native	Province	(N)	(%)
Central	Henan	5	2.64
	Hubei	10	5.29
	Hunan	8	4.23
	Jiangxi	2	1.06
East	Anhui	5	2.64
	Fujian	2	1.06
	Jiangsu	25	13.23
	Shandong	24	12.70
	Shanghai	3	1.59
	Taiwan	1	0.53
	Zhejiang	14	7.41
North	Beijing	4	2.12
	Hebei	22	11.64
	Inner Mongolia	1	0.53
	Shanxi	7	3.70
	Tianjin	4	2.12
Northeast	Heilongjiang	2	1.06
	Jilin	8	4.23
	Liaoning	7	3.70
Northwest	Gansu	1	0.53
	Ningxia	0	0.00
	Qinghai	0	0.00
	Shaanxi	3	1.59
	Xinjiang	2	1.06
South	Hainan	0	0.00
	Guangdong	4	2.12
	Guangxi	1	0.53
Southwest	Guizhou	1	0.53
	Sichuan	9	4.76
	Xizang	1	0.53
	Yunnan	2	1.06
Unknown		11	5.82
Total		189	100.00

SOURCE: Zang (1993). © 1993 by The Regents of the
University of California. Reprinted from *Asian Survey*, Vol.
33, No. 8, August 1993, pp. 794–795, by permission of the
Regents.

cial, municipal, and county levels over a wide range of political and economic activities, including personnel appointments, foreign and domestic supply, trade and investment decisions, price setting, and the collection of government revenues.

The devolution of authority in China is further enhanced by the fact that—unlike in the pre-reform period—many provincial and local bureaucratic technocrats are now native to the areas they govern.[23]

Moreover, such localism is reinforced by the fact that Beijing now only formally appoints subnational leaders down to the level of provincial vice governor. These changes ended the past practice of the so-called "law of avoidance" in the Chinese government, marked by the placement of nonnatives in leading government and party posts as a means of ensuring loyalty to the center. Such a practice became untenable in the face of the reform effort, which required leaders to possess a more detailed knowledge of local economic and social conditions.[24]

As a result of these developments, provincial and local civilian leaders in China today are more able to evade, alter, or even defy central decisions and are far more likely to defend their area's interest against the center and other localities than at any other time in the history of the People's Republic. The growing authority of provincial and local leaders is reflected in their overall increased role in the central elite.[25]

---

[23]For example, by the early nineties, over 70 percent of provincial leaders had devoted their entire careers to the provinces where they held their current posts. See Xiaowei Zang, "Provincial Elite in Post-Mao China," *Asian Survey*, Vol. 31, No. 6, June 1991, p. 516.

[24]Li and Bachman (1989), p. 86. It should be noted, however, that this trend has been at least partly reversed in recent years, as Beijing attempts to regain some of its past controls over local decisions by increasing the number of outsiders placed in critical subnational posts. See Huang Yasheng, "Central-Local Relations in China During the Reform Era: The Economic and Institutional Dimensions," unpublished paper, March 1995. However, on balance, the overall trend toward greater localism in personnel and decisionmaking authority still appears to hold true, especially as compared with the early and mid eighties.

[25]Sutter et. al. (1993), p. 10, and Susan Shirk, *The Political Logic of Economic Reform in China*, University of California Press, Berkeley, 1993, p. 337. Sutter points out that six provincial and municipal leaders were added to the Politburo at the Fourteenth Party Congress, marking ". . . the largest increase in such officials since the Cultural Revolution." Similarly, the proportion of Central Committee members representing

MILITARY LEADERS

Any attempt to understand leadership trends and features in China must take into account the role of the Chinese military. This critical institution serves as the ultimate guarantor of social order and the defender of the communist regime. It has also served as the key arbiter of power among the top elite and as an influential player in the formulation of domestic and foreign policies.[26]

China's military leadership has experienced major changes in composition and outlook under the reforms. This presents significant implications for the future scope and extent of military involvement in critical areas affecting China's long-term domestic stability and regional stance. Three closely interrelated trends and features are especially important:

• Heightened professionalism and attention to military modernization, tempered by a continued potential for involvement in elite politics

• The existence of several unresolved institutional concerns, many arising from military modernization and economic reform

• The emergence of divergent views toward contacts with the West, including a highly conservative variant of patriotic nationalism.

Military Professionalism and a Focus on Modernization

Parallel to the above changes in the civilian party and state leaderships, a new generation of more professional military leaders has also emerged during the past decade, largely replacing the military politicians of the revolutionary generation.[27] These officers are younger, better educated, and more professionally trained than in

---

local regions rose from 25 percent at the Thirteenth Congress (of 1987) to over 60 percent at the Fourteenth Congress.

[26]For an extended defense of this point, see Swaine (1992).

[27]It should be noted, however, that, although formally retired, several military elders retain considerable influence over leadership and other issues. This factor will be discussed in greater detail below.

the past.[28] Most have passed through one of the increasing number of China's military academies and institutes, where a much greater stress is placed on purely military skills, as opposed to political correctness. Hence, this emergent leadership generally denigrates the direct relevance of ideology to military affairs, while recognizing the need for civilian control over military forces. Moreover, as in the civilian sphere, individual members of China's emerging generation of military leaders possess far fewer political resources than their predecessors and hence are less able to serve as key power brokers or policy advocates than powerful military figures have done in the past. Equally important, on the organizational level, Chinese officers now command a military structure with little capacity to intervene *autonomously* in elite politics. Specifically, many changes in military structure, process, and personnel selection, most inaugurated under the reforms, have served to eliminate the ability of central or regional leaders to independently mobilize forces for political ends, as part of a factional leadership struggle.[29]

As a result of these and other developments, Chinese military officers today display both a greater sense of mission separate from the party and a much greater resistance to involvement in domestic political

---

[28]At least 67 percent of the military elite in the Fourteenth Central Committee and 75 percent of an "extended officer pool of 224" identified in 1988 have received higher education. In addition, over 30 percent of military Central Committee members have worked as presidents of, or other administrators in, military academies or technical schools. See Li Cheng and Lynn White, "The Army in the Succession to Deng Xiaoping: Familiar Fealties and Technocratic Trends," *Asian Survey*, Vol. 33, No. 8, August 1993, p. 761.

[29]The demise of such "independent kingdoms" resulted from a variety of factors. First, the commanders of China's seven military regions do not have the authority to independently order the units under their command into action. Only the Central Military Commission (CMC) in Beijing, the supreme party organ directing the military, has the authority to issue such orders. Second, senior officers at the higher levels of the military hierarchy have been frequently and extensively reshuffled since the early eighties as part of an intensified application of the above-mentioned "law of avoidance," thus undermining their ability to establish unit-based or geographically based political factions. Third, the PLA General Political Department, in consultation with the CMC leadership, formally appoints all regional officers of main force units at the level of divisional commander and above. Fourth, the closely cooperative, often interlocking party-army leadership structures of the past have been replaced by two essentially separate elites, as indicated by the above discussion of the emerging civilian leadership. Finally, central control over regional units has been furthered by the strengthening—since the Tiananmen incident—of the military's political control apparatus. For further details on all these points, see Swaine (1992).

affairs than their predecessors. This trend suggests an increasing orientation toward purely nationalistic—rather than socialist or even general social welfare—objectives and interests among most emerging military leaders, thus striking a parallel with the trend toward patriotic nationalism in the civilian leadership mentioned above. Moreover, the detachment of the military from politics is reflected in the fact that, since the end of the Cultural Revolution in the seventies, military leaders have all but disappeared from the formal ranks of party and government leadership at all levels (see Figure 2.1).[30] It is also reflected in the type of officers recently chosen to fill top leadership posts at the center. For example, the current heads of the military's three central departments (the General Staff Department (GSD), the General Political Department (GPD), and the General Logistics Department (GLD)) are professional combat officers with extensive experience at the regional levels, much weaker factional bases than their predecessors, and little prior involvement in party and state organs of rule.[31]

An indication of the resistance of the bulk of military officers to continued political involvement by their colleagues was provided by the removal of Yang Shangkun and Yang Baibing from power at the Fourteenth Party Congress, noted above. This action was apparently supported by the mainstream military. Both men had reportedly alienated many prominent party and military leaders. Senior and retired officers in particular were worried about the Yangs' increasing influence within both central and regional military organs, and Yang Baibing's increased stress on politics in the military was seen as undermining efforts at professionalization. Following the removal of the Yangs, two very senior generals, Liu Huaqing and Zhang Zhen,

---

[30]However, within the party Central Committee, this trend might be undergoing a reversal. The Fourteenth Central Committee contains nearly 200 military officers, over 20 percent of the total. This is the highest percentage of military representatives since 1969.

[31]In 1992, former Jinan Military Region (MR) Commander Zhang Wannian replaced Chi Haotian as PLA Chief of Staff. General Fu Quanyou, commander of the Lanzhou MR, took over control of the General Logistics Department from Zhao Nanqi, who became president of the influential Academy of Military Sciences. General Yu Yongbo was promoted from deputy director to director of the GPD. All three officers were also elevated to serve as regular members of the CMC Standing Committee, and subsequently promoted to the rank of full generals. Generals Zhang and Fu in particular served in several regional commands.

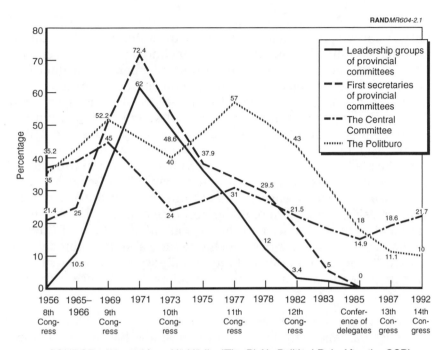

RAND*MR604-2.1*

SOURCE: Adapted from Yü Yü-lin, "The PLA's Political Role After the CCP's Thirteenth National Congress: Continuity and Change," *Issues & Studies*, Vol. 24, No. 9, September 1988, p. 21; and "The Fourteenth Party Congress: In Session," *China News Analysis*, November 1, 1992, pp. 7, 11, 12.

Figure 2.1—The Percentage of Military Cadres in the CCP's Politburo, Central Committee, and Provincial Committee

were brought out of semi-retirement and promoted to the Politburo Standing Committee and the CMC, respectively.[32] This was done largely to reassure both retired and serving military leaders that competent, trustworthy, and professional officers were now in charge of relations with the party, and to demonstrate military support for the more reformist civilian leadership appointed during the Congress.[33]

---

[32]General Liu was already a CMC member before the Party Congress.

[33]The appointment of Generals Liu Huaqing and Zhang Zhen to high party posts also marks the consolidation of an apparent coalition between the two most cohesive and dominant leadership factions within the military, largely centered on elements of the

In place of politics, the attention of China's emerging professional officer corps is now focused primarily on military modernization through continued economic reform, technological advancement, and improvements in force structure and operational doctrine. Military officers realize that Chinese conventional forces are extremely backward in many critical areas—especially when compared with their Western counterparts—and ill-suited to cope with the more complex and diverse challenges posed by a post–Cold War strategic environment.[34] Hence, they believe that enormous efforts must be made to "catch up" militarily with the West, and with industrialized countries in Asia, especially Japan. This belief not only stems from a desire to ensure China's future security but also reflects an increasing recognition of the importance of military strength for national pride and unity and the overall enhancement of China's regional and global stature.[35] Such views are also undoubtedly supported by the small number of retired military elders of the revolutionary generation who still wield considerable influence over military affairs.

Despite enormous changes, however, the Chinese military still retains several important links with the past and has also developed some new features that together suggest its continued connection to politics. As indicated above, the Chinese political-military system remains largely under the ultimate control of a small number of retired and "semi-retired" party and military elders. As long-standing leaders, these men possess many personal and professional connec-

---

former 2nd and 3rd Field Army systems. Both field armies enjoyed close historical ties before 1949. More important, their most senior surviving leaders have been strongly supportive of military reform and modernization since the eighties, and each has important links to the rising generation of younger military leaders. For further details, see Swaine (1992).

[34]See the final section of this chapter for a discussion of these new strategic requirements confronting the PLA. Also see Michael D. Swaine, "Strategic Appraisal: China," in Zalmay Khalilzad (ed.,) *Strategic Appraisal 1995*; RAND, forthcoming.

[35]For further discussions of these and related points, see Michael D. Swaine, "The Modernization of the Chinese People's Liberation Army: Prospects and Implications for Northeast Asia," *NBR Analysis*, Vol. 5, No. 3, October 1994; Harlan W. Jencks, *From Muskets to Missiles: Politics and Professionalism in the Chinese Army, 1945–1981*, Westview Press, Boulder, Colorado, 1982; Ellis Joffe, "China's Military: The PLA in Internal Politics," *Problems of Communism*, Vol. 24, November/December 1975, pp. 1–12; and Richard J. Latham and Kenneth W. Allen, "Defense Reform in China: The PLA Air Force," *Problems of Communism*, Vol. 40, May–June 1991, pp. 30–50.

tions to one another and to the current senior military leadership, particularly those central and regional commanders who previously served under elders in military units or regions. These high-level links are also important because of the downward ties that likely exist between many senior commanders and their former subordinates in leadership posts at the regional and army levels. Moreover, such links are probably augmented by additional factional ties among active officers based upon service arms and military academies.

Such informal associations suggest that Chinese military forces could be used, *under extreme circumstances,* for political ends, despite the changes noted above. This danger is increased by two basic characteristics of the military command system: (a) it presents major irregularities in procedure and potential ambiguities in authority relationships; and (b) it permits direct access by a command center in Beijing to both army and division headquarters. These features could enable military and party elders and younger civilian successors in a post-elder setting to issue direct orders to factional associates among regional forces in a time of extreme crisis.[36] Thus, military forces could become drawn into the fray in a post-Deng succession contest. Alternatively, the military leadership might become completely paralyzed in such circumstances, due to an absence of clear directives from above and its own internal debates. In either worst case, the outcome for regime stability would almost certainly be disastrous.[37]

Unresolved Institutional Concerns

Although China's military elite is more unified in support of professional development and force modernization over involvement in politics and ideology, it is by no means free from tensions and concerns. Of greatest significance is a range of unresolved issues relating primarily to the military's institutional development. These include:

---

[36]For further details, see Swaine (1992). See also Michael D. Swaine, "Chinese Regional Forces as Political Actors," in Richard H. Yang et al. (eds.), *Chinese Regionalism: The Security Dimension,* Westview Press, Boulder, Colorado, 1994.

[37]See below for a more detailed discussion of these and other scenarios of military involvement in elite politics.

- Continued interference by political commissars in professional military matters such as personnel selection

- Low morale and corruption within the ranks

- Inadequate government funding in many critical areas relating to modernization

- The possibility of growing social unrest arising from the leadership transition or the process of economic reform

- Growing involvement in profit-making economic activities.

Most of these issues emerged in the eighties as a consequence of military modernization and economic reform, and some have been ignored or only weakly addressed by the Deng Xiaoping regime. The contrasting interests and duties of commanders and political commissars have produced problems within the military since at least the early days of the communist government. However, this situation reportedly reached a critical level in the eighties, largely as a consequence of the unprecedented changes wrought by the military reform effort. While a much greater emphasis has been placed upon the use of purely professional, as opposed to political, criteria in many military areas, political commissars continue to exert a decisive influence over critical personnel decisions, including the recruitment, training, and promotion of officers and ordinary soldiers. Moreover, such decisions are sometimes made for highly personal reasons unrelated to both political and professional considerations. To many (especially younger) officers, the influence exerted by commissars over personnel decisions is at best highly inappropriate and at worst extremely corrupting to the creation of a modern, professional military establishment. Consequently, some officers have argued for a wholesale downgrading of the political commissar system.[38] Although these views have reportedly been communicated to the highest levels of the Chinese leadership at times, little action has been taken, partly because of a concern over the weakening of party

---

[38]This does not imply a rejection of party control over the military, however. Most (especially senior) officers apparently believe that mechanisms to ensure obedience to the party should be preserved under a curtailed commissar system.

control,[39] and partly because of fears that such a change would reflect adversely on Deng Xiaoping, a former political commissar.

The second and third concerns are closely related, i.e., low military morale and rising corruption have become especially acute problems in recent years because of the generally low level of funding available for troop support.[40] Other significant causes also exist, however, including (a) the declining attractiveness of military service compared with the more lucrative gains offered by the market-driven civilian economy; (b) the damage to the military's prestige and status within society caused by its violent acts against Chinese citizens during the May–June 1989 Tiananmen incident; and (c) the corrupting effect of the military's expanding involvement in profit-making economic activities (discussed in greater detail below). These and other threats to military élan and discipline are prompting increased pressures within the military for additional government revenues and more intensive "morale-building" efforts, many keyed to the theme of patriotic nationalism discussed above. It has also increased pressures for significant reductions in the number and size of combat units and other structural changes designed to create a more efficient and less costly military establishment. However, many of these (and other) proposed solutions to the military's morale and corruption problems have generated considerable controversy within both military and civilian leadership circles.

Concerns about severe domestic unrest resulting from future internal leadership disputes or economic reform is quite common among officers, given the military's pivotal responsibility for social and political order. Indeed, the professionalization of the Chinese military has led to a much greater focus on its institutional role as *the* guarantor of national unity and order over its past function as an agent of revolutionary change, so evident during the Maoist period. This feature could eventually prompt unified military intervention in

---

[39]This concern will likely increase after the passing of Deng Xiaoping, as a relatively "weak" civilian successor leadership seeks to maintain effective controls over the military.

[40]Concerns over future levels of government funding available to the military are motivated, in turn, by broader difficulties confronting the economic reform effort and the PLA's apparent desire to increase the pace of military modernization, both discussed further below.

politics, and it could also generate conflict within the ranks. For example, the fear of prolonged leadership strife resulting from the succession process has led some officers to voice support privately for the appointment of several senior military leaders to the Politburo Standing Committee after Deng's death.[41] Other officers resist such an action, however, for fear that it would lead to increased military involvement in elite politics, thereby reversing recent trends. Moreover, fears of social unrest associated with the continued marketization and privatization of the Chinese economy (e.g., unemployment, corruption, and crime) has reportedly led some officers to argue for a slower pace of economic reform. It has also led to arguments favoring increased political controls over the populace. For example, many military officers (along with some civilian leaders and intellectuals) desire more aggressive government action to reduce the large number of jobless and impoverished peasants who are descending on China's cities in search of employment or better wages. This "floating population" of nearly one hundred million peasants is seen as a potential threat to social and political order.

Military involvement in a wide range of business activities, mentioned above, arguably constitutes another important threat to the unity of China's officer corps and to its detachment from politics. The relatively low priority accorded to military versus civilian development under the reforms has forced the Chinese military to generate a significant proportion of its own revenues in order to fund its ambitious modernization and professionalization effort.[42] This has produced a growing trend toward extensive military participation in money-making activities in a variety of areas. Throughout China, increasing numbers of military factories are converting to civilian production while numerous military units of all types are establishing profit-oriented enterprises, many in the foreign trade sector. The dynamic coastal regions in particular are increasingly serving as sites for such military enterprises.[43] In addition, many individual military

---

[41]This proposal is also motivated by the perceived need for a military voice in senior leadership organs on critical policy issues relevant to military modernization.

[42]Details of this effort are provided in Chapter Five.

[43]For further information on the military's growing involvement in profit-making activities, see Tai Ming Cheung, "Elusive Ploughshares," *Far Eastern Economic Review,* October 14, 1993, pp. 70–71; Tai Ming Cheung, "Making Money, Not War," *China Trade Report,* August, 1993, p. 5; Tai Ming Cheung, "Profits over Professionalism: The

officers are engaging in various private business pursuits to supplement their personal and family incomes, often without the knowledge or permission of higher authorities.

The Chinese military's extensive and expanding foray into capitalist endeavors is only dimly understood by outside observers; in fact, few, if any, Chinese insiders understand its full dimensions and significance. For example, little information is known about the amount of revenue generated by the military's business activities, its specific use, and its method of supervision and control by the Chinese leadership.[44] As a result, the long-term consequences of this growing trend can only be surmised. Nevertheless, interviews with Chinese officers and other knowledgeable sources suggest that this phenomenon is generating significant concerns within the Chinese military that could have serious implications for the future unity of the military and its role in domestic politics and foreign policy.

Most observers agree that the military's business involvement has generally served to exacerbate personalistic interests and corrupt tendencies within the ranks. Furthermore, concerns over such developments might be producing a division between those officers who place a priority on professionalism and view business activities as corrosive to the creation of a modern fighting force and those officers who gain greatly from such activities and view them as an essential foundation for continued military reform and development.[45]

PLA's Economic Activities and the Impact on Military Unity," in Richard H. Yang et al. (eds.), *Chinese Regionalism: The Security Dimension*, Westview, Boulder, Colorado, 1994, pp. 85–110; Sheila Tefft, "China's Military Grapples with Conversion," *The Christian Science Monitor*, February 7, 1994, p. 4, and Thomas J. Bickford, "The Chinese Military and Its Business Operations," *Asian Survey*, Vol. 34, No. 5, May 1995, pp. 460–474.

[44]Most estimates of the revenues generated by the military's business activities cite a figure of approximately $5 billion to $7 billion per year, but the basis for such a calculation is rarely spelled out. Second, most observers agree that these revenues are primarily used at the local unit level to support basic troop needs (e.g., housing and food), and not to procure weapons. However, one might argue that this permits more government revenues to be used for procurement purposes. Third, observers generally agree that most business activities are under the formal supervision of the military's logistics apparatus, but how closely this reflects the actual pattern of control is impossible to determine.

[45]Of course, a large number of officers probably fall between these two extremes, as supporters of both a more professional military and at least a certain level of business involvement. Moreover, the use of the general term "professionalism" is somewhat

The former individuals probably tend to favor a greater reliance by the military on central government appropriations to support the modernization effort, while the latter stress greater reliance on localist, reform-oriented, military-led enterprises and expanded military involvement in the private economy, especially the foreign trade sector.[46]

As in the case of the civilian leadership, these internal tensions are further complicated by the fact that the family members of many senior and retired Chinese leaders are involved in the military's economic activities. Many of these individuals oversee China's major arms sales companies, for example.[47] As noted above, the influence of this subgroup among the princelings, heretofore limited in nature, could increase dramatically after the passing of the princelings' parents. For example, many in this subgroup could provide crucial support for those professionals in the military favoring the increased use of arms sales over civilian business activities as a means of maintaining adequate levels of funding for the modernization effort.

Some knowledgeable observers of the Chinese military believe that such differences constitute *the* most significant potential threat to future military unity. The danger posed by this issue would become particularly acute if it were to bring about a split among the most senior military leaders. There are signs that the party leadership has recognized the political dangers posed by increased military involvement in profit-oriented activities and has begun to curtail or eliminate them.[48] However, it remains to be seen whether such efforts will produce the intended results.

---

inappropriate in this context, since officers on both sides of this issue should be regarded as more professional in many ways than their predecessors, as noted above. The term is intended to denote a particularly strong resistance to nonmilitary (and especially commercial) activities.

[46]Cheung (1994).

[47]John Lewis, Hua Di, and Xue Litai, "Beijing's Defense Establishment: Solving the Arms-Export Enigma," *International Security*, Vol. 15, No. 4, Spring 1991, pp. 87–109. Also, see the appendix to this report.

[48]See, for example, Lu Yu-shan, "CPC Prohibits Armed Forces from Engaging in Business," in *Tangtai* (Hong Kong), No. 35, February 15, 1994, pp. 14–15, in *FBIS-CHI*, February 7, 1994, pp. 23–24.

Differing Views Toward the West and Increasing Conservative Nationalist Sentiments

In addition to the above institutional problems affecting the military, notable differences also exist within the Chinese officer corps over at least one major policy issue of direct relevance to this report, i.e., relations with the West.[49] Interviews with military insiders and articles on security strategy appearing in military publications suggest that most military officers favor a continuation of the cautious, balanced, cooperative/competitive approach to the West that constitutes part of the current mainstream civilian view of China's external relations, discussed in Chapters Three and Five.[50]

However, this dominant viewpoint has been challenged in recent years by a large and growing number of military officers who believe that the West, led by the United States, is trying to weaken or fragment China by promoting domestic dissent, separatism, and independence activities among the populace. Many of these individuals (reportedly including several retired military elders) are disappointed by the poor results attained through past cooperation with the United States and are angered by Washington's growing pressure on trade, human rights, and proliferation issues, as well as arms sales to Taiwan. Moreover, many military (and some civilian) strategists believe that the United States is secretly encouraging Taiwan's supposed bid for independence. As a result, a growing number of these strategists reportedly insist that China will eventually need to use military means to preempt such a strategy and reclaim the island.[51]

---

[49]In general, the military viewpoints toward the West presented in this section largely parallel the three intellectual approaches toward Chinese security interests and resulting strategy outlined in Chapter Three.

[50]This observation also coincides with the general findings of a delegation of former high-level U.S. military and Department of Defense officials who met with senior members of the Chinese officer corps during May–June 1994. In these meetings, Chinese military leaders stressed the existence of both tensions and common interests with the United States, which was viewed as ". . . a diplomatic and political challenge (to China), but not a military threat." For further details, see Robert S. McNamara et al., *Sino-American Military Relations: Mutual Responsibilities in the Post–Cold War Era*, National Committee China Policy Series, No. Nine, New York, November 1994.

[51]Some mainstream strategists (both civilian and military) strenuously reject this view, however, arguing that U.S. influence on Taiwan is declining and that a military "solution" to the problem would likely lead at worst to conflict with the United States and at best to a prolonged military occupation of a hostile population.

Thus, some military analysts reportedly favor a much tougher stand toward the West—and the United States in particular—and increased reliance on Russia for future military equipment and technology. Moreover, because of such perceptions, many of these officers apparently feel a growing need to accelerate the pace of military modernization, to provide China with greater leverage in the Asia-Pacific region and a stronger deterrent against various U.S. (and possibly Japanese) pressures. In particular, some officers argue that the modernization and expansion of China's maritime capabilities (both naval and air) should take precedence over improvements in its capability to defend against threats from the interior of Asia.[52]

These hardline views are reinforced by the growing influence within China's officer corps of a highly conservative variant of patriotic nationalism. While sharing the state-centered image of a wealthy and powerful China basic to the above-outlined civilian notion of patriotic nationalism, this viewpoint places a particular stress upon certain xenophobic and chauvinistic elements, centering on a pronounced distrust of the West and a strong desire for China to reclaim its historical role as the dominant power in Asia through the development of a far more potent military force.

Such views share many basic assumptions of a broader intellectual school of nationalist thought known to outside observers as "neoconservatism" and mentioned above in footnote 11. This school of thought asserts that the stability, unity, and spirit of Chinese society and government are gravely threatened by a wide range of alleged social, political, and economic ills largely associated with the reforms, including the emergence of an ideological and moral vacuum, the absence of a genuinely public-spirited government protective of the most impoverished segments of society, the steady disintegration of the public sector of the economy and its replacement by a rapacious and corrupt private sector, the general lack of discipline among most socioeconomic classes, a fear of China's growing mass of uprooted, discontented peasantry,[53] and the supposedly pernicious

---

[52]Further details on the implications of this viewpoint for China's foreign policy stance are discussed in Chapter Five.

[53]Hence, the above-mentioned demand within certain military circles for greater controls over China's "floating population" is usually associated with this view.

social and economic influence of foreign cultural and economic elements. To cope with such supposedly enormous threats to China's political and social order, proponents of neo-conservatism enunciate a militarily and economically strong "populist authoritarian" form of central government designed to reinstill the values of a unified moral order, ensure the existence of a strong public sector in the economy, and significantly limit contacts with the "predatory" West.[54]

In contrast to both the mainstream view and its hardline variant, a smaller but significant contingent within the Chinese officer corps takes a much more positive view toward the West and the United States in particular. This viewpoint, also found among civilian strategists and officials (see Chapter Three), is largely concentrated among younger, less senior, and more professional military officers. Although intensely patriotic, these "progressives" are disappointed with the deterioration in Sino-U.S. relations since the Tiananmen incident. They recognize that successful military modernization and a secure, stable China will depend upon continued close links with the outside and a more positive relationship with the advanced industrialized countries of the West. Among some officers, such foreign policy views may even be combined with support for a limited degree of domestic political liberalization. In fact, some observers suggest that the lower ranks of the officer corps in particular are now widely infected by a variety of radical ideas, including the notion of a national army loyal to the government first and foremost and free from party control. Officers at these levels are apparently regarded with considerable suspicion by both the mainstream and conservative central party and military leaderships, however,[55] and are thought to provide the largest number of supporters of so-called "anti-party groups" within the military. As a result, they are reportedly subjected to strict surveillance and control. Although certainly

---

[54]For a useful summary of the major tenets of neo-conservatism, and its historical emergence during the reform period, see Joseph Fewsmith, "Neoconservatism and the End of the Dengist Era," unpublished paper presented at a UCLA-sponsored conference on "China After Deng," held March 11, 1995.

[55]One could argue that the notion of a national army is implicit in the concept of patriotic nationalism found within both senior and lower ranks. However, most proponents of the mainstream and "neo-conservative" viewpoints within the military appear to maintain a strong emphasis on party control of the military and the government.

in an extreme minority today (especially among senior officers), the influence of this viewpoint could increase in the post-Deng era.[56]

At present, differences among the above three viewpoints toward the West are largely eclipsed by the military's common support for continued economic reform and defense modernization and the patriotic nationalist views held by virtually all military officers. However, this could change in the future, especially in the broader context of a succession struggle or a declining economy. Details regarding several possible scenarios are presented in Chapter Five.

IMPLICATIONS: A MORE UNIFIED LEADERSHIP, BUT WITH INTERNAL TENSIONS

The above trends and features suggest that China's leadership over the next 10–15 years will display at least three major characteristics:

*   Movement toward a strongly pro-reform collective civilian leadership structure, but with the potential for significant internal splits, most likely during the medium to long term, and probably over economic policy

*   The intensification of a serious imbalance in the distribution of power between the center and the periphery, threatening efforts by the successor leadership to implement effective policies

*   A potential for increasing (and possibly adverse) military influence over the civilian leadership, despite a trend toward military detachment from politics, accompanied by greater leadership support overall for more patriotic nationalist (and possibly hardline "neo-conservative") policies.

A More Cooperative Civilian Leadership?[57]

The emergence of an unprecedented level of policy consensus within China's bureaucratic-technocracy, the limited political and organi-

---

[56]For further details, see Swaine (1992).

[57]This subsection draws heavily on the work of David Bachman. See, especially, "The Limits to Leadership in China," in "The Future of China," *NBR Analysis*, Vol. 3, No. 3, August 1992, pp. 23–35.

zational resources held by each member of this new elite, and the pressures on the central leadership posed by increasing provincial and regional authority and the threat of widespread social disorder together provide the basis for the emergence of a relatively stable collective leadership structure after the passing of Deng Xiaoping and the other remaining members of the revolutionary generation. Each member of the successor leadership almost certainly realizes that an open and paralyzing struggle among them could threaten the survival of the communist regime and thus lead to their common demise. Moreover, the shared political weaknesses of the successors, along with the highly fragmented and increasingly decentralized nature of the Chinese policy process,[58] mean that *any* aspiring leader will almost certainly require support from a coalition of his colleagues and the cooperation or acquiescence of many of the major party and state bureaucracies to attain and maintain power. This will necessitate making promises and generating rewards to a broad and diverse group of individuals and institutions, which will, in turn, require continued sound economic performance. Also, these factors suggest that few incentives will exist for any leader to make sudden, major shifts in policy direction, or to independently opt for personal support from the military or particular groups within the officer corps. In the highly uncertain political environment of the post-elder era, either action could expose an individual or group of individuals to potential attack from colleagues.[59]

---

[58]In many areas, policy "decisions" largely result from an ongoing series of smaller, reinforcing decisions involving extensive bargaining among relevant organizations and individuals at every level of government, each of which wields separate resources and exhibits distinctive interests. Extensive cooperation and coordination among different functional bureaucratic systems, hierarchical levels, and geographic regions are thus required for the system to function, especially concerning major economic policy issues (see Chapter Four for more on this point). Moreover, such a structurally fragmented, incremental policy environment facilitates obstructionist activities by those middle-level party and government bureaucrats at the center and in the localities who fear that further reforms will diminish their power, prestige, and perquisites. Under such conditions, politically weak successors at the top will need to cooperate in many issue areas to ensure even a modicum of policy results, especially in the economic arena.

[59]Cooperation among the civilian successor leadership is also suggested by the fact that a rough balance of power apparently exists among the four leading contenders (Jiang Zemin, Li Peng, Zhu Rongji, and Qiao Shi). As suggested above, each man controls a major institution and at least one major policy arena (i.e., Jiang heads the party structure and leads several important policy groups, Li heads the State Council and probably leads the foreign affairs policy group (assuming he has not lost that post to

At the same time, however, certain other characteristics of political power in China indicate that a collective leadership structure will likely prove difficult to maintain, especially over the long term. The absence of institutionalized and regularized structures and processes for transferring and wielding power, China's long history of individual rule, and the general emphasis in Chinese culture (and communist ideology) on a monistic political structure serve to obstruct the creation of enduring bonds of trust among leaders. Thus, strong incentives will remain for any successor to seek to coopt or oust his erstwhile colleagues and consolidate sole power, thereby provoking a general leadership struggle. Moreover, this danger is likely increased by the existence of several significant contenders for power outside the formal leadership structure, such as Zhao Ziyang and Yang Shangkun.

These factors suggest that power motives alone might precipitate severe leadership conflict leading to regime instability, especially in the period immediately following the death of Deng Xiaoping. On the other hand, the above policy-related issues and challenges facing the emerging civilian and military leaderships imply that several types of policy problems could also initiate (or aggravate) tensions and conflict among the successor leadership over the medium to long term. Indeed, the crucial importance of continued economic development to social stability and government legitimacy, the different approaches to economic reform evident among the emerging civilian leadership, and the existence of several major obstacles to any deepening of the reform effort (outlined in Chapter Four) suggest that conflict over economic issues would serve as the most likely catalyst for such a policy-based leadership struggle.

Whether or not various power and/or policy machinations eventually overcome the strong pressures toward cooperation within the successor leadership and produce significant political instability will largely depend on factors operating essentially outside the realm of central elite politics, including the future state of the economy, the political role played by the military, the influence of provincial and

---

Jiang Zemin), Zhu heads the economic policy arena, and Qiao Shi controls the National People's Congress and exerts major influence over intelligence activities and political/legal affairs.

regional leaders outside Beijing, and the actions of foreign governments. These factors are assessed below and in Chapter Five.[60]

Increasingly Unbalanced Center-Periphery Relationship

Changes in the provincial and regional composition of China's central elite, the emergence of more regionally oriented local officials
and business elites, and the overall increasing ability of localities to
evade central directives together present several potential problems
for the long-term stability and unity of China's leadership. On the
administrative level, the latter trend in particular could undermine
the ability of the central leadership to develop and implement coor-
dinated national policies designed to avoid severe social and other
difficulties during the critical final stages of the economic reform effort, described in Chapter Four. Moreover, the virtual nullification of
the past "law of avoidance" in selecting provincial and subprovincial
civilian officials suggests that more independent localists, including
private business elites, could eventually obtain political power at
various subnational levels, thereby worsening existing confrontations between the center and the periphery. This problem is further
aggravated by the low level of representation in central political leadership organs afforded to officials from the dynamic southern
provinces and the relatively high level of representation enjoyed by
cadres from the East. As suggested above, such a trend presents the
possibility of a major geographical imbalance between political and
economic power in China. This is discussed further in Chapter Four.

Overall, regime stability may thus ultimately depend, over at least the
medium term, on (a) the establishment of strong coalitions between
central and local officials that could counteract the centrifugal forces
affecting central-peripheral relations, or (b) the emergence of a central leadership that more accurately represents the changing distribution of power and influence among subnational elites. Over the
long term, however, such developments could also become counter-
productive and produce a growing confrontation over economic
policy between an alliance of radical central reformers, southern
provincial and local officials, and private business elites on the one

---

[60]However, as pointed out in Chapter One, the actions of foreign governments are not
discussed extensively in this report.

hand, and socialist bureaucrats, conservative military leaders, and subnational officials of the eastern—and perhaps inland—provinces on the other. The formation of such broad-based, opposing alliances would become especially likely in the context of a stagnant or declining economy.

Increasing Military Influence, and Possible Intervention in Politics

China's officer corps will likely provide significant support for a co-operative civilian leadership structure in Beijing. However, unlike in the past, such support will derive largely from pragmatic considerations linked to the military's desire for continued economic growth and the maintenance of political and social order, not personal ties between military officers and party leaders. The military's likely inclination to support the central political leadership is arguably further reinforced by the *strengthening* of the "law of avoidance" among senior regional and provincial military leaders, noted above. This trend lessens the political danger to Beijing presented by the increasing localization of subnational civilian elites.

However, military support could easily lead to extensive military influence over a future leadership's policy agenda and direction. The common political weaknesses of the civilian successors (and their likely fear of direct military intervention in politics), the military's above-mentioned institutional concerns, and its strong preference for a sustained rate of defense modernization indicate that even a stable civilian leadership will probably encounter increasing pressures to placate the armed forces on key domestic and foreign policy issues. This will prove especially likely if senior retired military elders remain active after Deng's passing. Even without the presence of such individuals, however, China's civilian successor leadership will likely face a growing necessity to listen closely to military views on a variety of matters and to generally incorporate senior military officers more fully into the policymaking process, both formally and informally. Such a development could eventually lead to the emergence of a collective civil-military leadership structure, despite the greater apolitical inclinations of the emerging professional officer corps.

More direct, and possibly destabilizing, patterns of military involvement in leadership politics and policymaking are also possible. First, a protracted power struggle over the succession to Deng could eventually lead to efforts by individual civilian leaders to reach out to various groups within the military for partisan support, as has occurred in past political crises in China. In this instance, certain civilian leaders might stress highly nationalistic themes to gain support from both mainstream and hardline officers. Second, the above-mentioned institutional concerns of the military could aggravate policy tensions among the top military elite and between the military and civilian party leadership, especially if declining state revenues and rapidly increasing demands for public expenditures greatly limit the ability of the government to finance military modernization. The leadership conflicts produced by this (and the preceding) scenario could eventually split the military (at both central and local levels), derail the succession process, and seriously threaten the stability of the communist regime. Third, protracted post-Deng succession struggles or escalating policy conflicts among contending factions within the party leadership could prompt the military to intervene in leadership politics *on a unified basis*, to assure political stability, social order, and continued economic advance. Many knowledgeable Chinese and foreign observers argue that this form of military intervention is, on balance, the most likely, given the reduced ability and willingness of the military to become involved in civilian factional politics and the increased attention of a more professional officer corps to the maintenance of national unity and government stability.

Finally, *any* form of miltary involvement in elite politics will likely accelerate the trend toward more patriotic nationalist, and possibly "neo-conservative," policies, given the growing presence of such views within Chinese military leadership circles.

The above potential leadership developments and their implications for China's regional behavior over the long term are associated with several possible alternative Chinese security approaches to the Asia-Pacific region, discussed in Chapter Five.

Chapter Three

SOCIAL AND INTELLECTUAL TRENDS

Three broad categories of social and intellectual trends and features have the greatest implications for future adverse change within China:

- Increasing rates of urbanization

- Popular attitudes and beliefs toward politics and the state

- Specialist views on China's future security environment.

A UNIQUE PATTERN OF URBANIZATION

China has experienced extremely high levels of both urbanization and urban population growth during the reform period.[1] These developments may be generating major social problems in China, such as overcrowding, poverty, increased crime, greatly overburdened infrastructures, and environmental damage, all of which place enormous pressures on municipal and national governments. However, a closer examination of this phenomenon reveals that:

- Patterns of urbanization and urban population growth in China are highly distinctive, and should not be evaluated in the same manner as similar phenomena in other rapidly developing Third World countries.

---

[1] For details, see the companion study to this report, Michael D. Swaine and Courtney Purrington with Don Henry, Ashley Tellis, and James Winnefeld, *Asia's Changing Security Environment: Sources of Adversity for U.S. Policy*, RAND, forthcoming.

Several major differences are especially notable. First, unlike most other Asian countries, the Chinese government has vigorously promoted policies designed to limit the growth of large cities and encourage the growth of intermediate cities and towns. Major mechanisms have included controls over internal migration and family size, land-use planning, the development of new coastal cities and special economic zones, the provision of essential services, and methods to encourage employment in small towns.[2] Moreover, such government policies have been intensified since the advent of the reform period, with a particular policy emphasis placed on the development of smaller towns and cities. This has resulted in a relatively controlled, spatially balanced, and decentralized pattern of urban development, in contrast to the accelerated, largely uncontrolled pattern of urbanization evident in most of the Third World. Thus, although China will tend to urbanize at an accelerating pace in the future, less than 50 percent of the population is expected to reside in urban areas by 2010, compared with much higher proportions of urban residents projected for many other rapidly growing Asian countries.

Second, China's unique pattern of urbanization results from certain special historical and economic conditions. For example, between 1977 and 1987, a significant part of the rapid increase in urban residents was due to the officially sanctioned return to urban areas of millions of persons sent to the countryside during the Cultural Revolution of 1966–1976. Many of these individuals returned to existing households and thus placed relatively lower pressures on urban housing. In addition, many other new urban dwellers are not permanent residents. Some are part of China's large, mobile "floating population," consisting of tens of millions of citizens who migrate to various urban areas in search of better paying jobs. Others are individual rural males who work and live in towns and cities to augment the income of their families, who remain in the countryside.

Finally, the level of urban population growth since the early eighties has been exaggerated statistically, because of several factors. For ex-

---

[2]G. Edward Ebanks and Chaoze Cheng, "China: A Unique Urbanization Model," *Asia-Pacific Population Journal*, Vol. 5, No. 3, 1990; and Ernesto M. Pernia, *Urbanization, Population Distribution and Economic Development in Asia*, Asian Development Bank, Economics and Development Resource Center, February 1993, p. 9.

ample, some of the rapid increase in the size of urban areas in the eighties is attributed to the establishment of entirely new towns, many inaugurated in 1984. Other increases resulted from the creation of new, larger boundaries for existing cities that included many formerly rural residents. As a result of these and other factors, ". . . the exact level of urban growth [has been] much lower than that shown by the statistical data."[3]

These and other factors certainly do not imply that urban areas are not increasing significantly in China, that China's total urban population is not enormous, and that the growth of urban areas does not have important implications for long-term political and social stability. However, they do suggest that the process of urbanization may not be as critical a factor in evaluating the future stability of political leadership in China as in other rapidly growing Asian economies, assuming that the Chinese government is able to continue with its present interventionist urban development policies. In other words, in an otherwise stable political environment, urbanization should not be regarded as a major independent cause of adverse domestic change in China.

POPULAR ATTITUDES AND BELIEFS

China's economic reform program and opening to the outside have wrought major changes in popular attitudes toward government and party authority and increased both the opportunities and the problems confronting many social elements. These developments are fundamentally altering the nature of state-society relations in China and the calculations of the political and military leadership. Most notably, such changes have raised the prospect of the emergence of an incipient civil society, as well as the danger of severe social disparities, that together present enormous implications for the country's future political structure and policy orientation, including its relations with the outside world. Several major trends are especially significant:

---

[3]Ebanks and Cheng (1990), pp. 33–36.

- Rising expectations of higher living standards among an increasing number of social classes, tempered by growing economic uncertainties and anxieties in some sectors and regions

- Widespread political cynicism, passivity, and low class consciousness among the mass of urban and rural dwellers, combined with signs of increasing nationalist pride in China's recent achievements

- The absence of genuinely representative social organizations to mediate between state and society

- A deep chasm between the attitudes and beliefs of the general populace and more politically aware social groups, reinforced by a popular aversion to social and political disorder.

Rising Expectations and Anxieties

Virtually every major social group in China has benefitted substantially from economic reform, including farmers and urban light and medium industrial workers and managers, the financial elite, entrepreneurs, most of the top political leadership, and much of the military. Such economic improvements have created strong expectations among most social classes (and especially China's growing economic elite of private entrepreneurs located primarily in the coastal areas) of continued high growth rates and improved living standards.[4] This fact, combined with the bankruptcy of Marxist ideology and the resulting erosion of party authority since the Cultural Revolution, has served to firmly peg the regime's future legitimacy to its ability to provide continued economic benefits for the populace. More narrowly, such trends are also producing a nascent urban middle class with increasing economic wealth and freedom and a growing interest in the further expansion of the market.

---

[4]Overholt (1993), pp. 93, 112. A survey conducted within a broad cross section of Chinese social groups indicates that most Chinese are pleased with the pace of the reforms, and that support for continued reform will exist as long as it is seen to produce clear benefits. See "Survey of Residents' 'Tolerance Level' for Reform," *Guanli Shijie* [Management World], No. 5, September 24, 1993, pp. 189–198, in *FBIS-CHI*, December 22, 1993.

At the same time, however, some social groups and areas of the country have encountered significant hardships as a result of the reforms or feel extremely uncertain about the future. Many urban workers in state enterprises are used to the security of a guaranteed job, low-cost housing, health care, and schooling for their children and feel threatened by the pressures and competition of the marketplace. In the countryside, some peasants are experiencing declines in income resulting from an adverse shift in the terms of trade for agricultural goods. In some instances, local cadres have misused funds earmarked to pay peasants for grain and levied illegal taxes and fees to invest or speculate in various private endeavors, prompting demonstrations and riots.[5] Many citizens in general are increasingly angered by the growing corruption of officials at all levels of the party and government. Regionally, elements of the population in areas that have traditionally benefitted most from the redistributive efforts of a strong central government (e.g., many less-developed inland provinces and border areas in the northwest and southwest) remain concerned about the future effect upon their lives of a weakened center. Overall, such attitudes are creating the basis for expanded levels of discontent about a further deepening of the reform effort.

Political Cynicism and Passivity, Combined with Increasing Nationalist Sentiments

While holding strong feelings of both hope and fear concerning the future, the majority of Chinese citizens remain politically passive and largely detached from any direct interest in government, even at the local level. In general, most of them have a very low perception of the effect of government on their lives, although many are acutely aware of its potential for destroying the gains of the past. Many urban citizens do not identify their interests with those of other members of their class or social stratum, focusing instead on their family or immediate neighborhood. Such attitudes are even more common in the countryside, where most classes live in self-contained social and political communities and often view the government as distant and largely irrelevant. This viewpoint is accentuated by the fact that

---

[5]Sutter et al. (1993), pp. 11–12.

the political and economic roles of the village party secretary, formerly the leading representative of state authority at the village level, have greatly declined under the reforms. Indeed, in general, party and government cadres throughout China increasingly exhibit a venal, self-serving mentality that adds to popular disillusionment with authority.[6]

However, such narrow, selfish, and apolitical behavior should not lead one to assume that Chinese citizens are indifferent toward their country's relationship with the outside world. On the contrary, rapid domestic economic growth, the expansion of Chinese economic and diplomatic ties with the outside, growing defense budgets, and the communist regime's increased emphasis on patriotic themes have combined to produce a more open expression of highly nationalistic views and emotions among the Chinese populace. Many ordinary citizens show an increasing level of pride in China's accomplishments under the reforms and in some cases express a strong desire to translate those accomplishments into more concerted efforts to redress past grievances and generally improve China's influence and stature in the international arena. Such beliefs have provided important support for the state-centered nationalist themes increasingly found within certain leadership and intellectual circles, including their more hardline, "neo-conservative" variant.

The Absence of Genuine Interest Groups

Few if any organizations or groups exist in China to address the above problems and features of Chinese society. Historically, the laboring classes and their allies (including industrial workers and most white collar workers) have exerted only minimal influence on the communist political system. They have been "represented" by the state-sanctioned (and generally passive) All-China Federation of Trade Unions (ACFTU) and have enjoyed only a very weak presence

---

[6]Lucian Pye, "China: Erratic State, Frustrated Society," *Foreign Affairs*, Vol. 69, No. 4, Fall 1990, pp. 56–74; "The Changing Roles of the Village Party Secretary," *China News Analysis*, No. 1488, July 1, 1993; Sutter et al. (1993), p. 12; and Andrew Nathan and Tianjin Shi, "Cultural Requisites for Democracy in China: Findings from a Survey," *Daedalus*, Vol. 122, No. 2, Spring 1993, pp. 95–123. In this survey, analyzed by Nathan and Shi, approximately 72 percent of Chinese citizens stated that both national and local governments had no effect on their daily lives (p. 104).

in government policy organs. In recent years, many new social organizations supportive of greater economic reform have emerged in China, including lateral socioeconomic associations of interest groups. Such organizations could *potentially* serve as more effective mechanisms for mediating social conflict and discontent and aggregating social attitudes to fashion policies that genuinely address the economic and other problems of Chinese society. Yet these reform-based associations are often politically disinterested or conservative in outlook, internally fragmented, and closely monitored by the government. Many are disbanded voluntarily or by force.[7] Hence, they do not as yet offer the prospect of serving as genuine intermediaries between state and society.

The Gap Between Political Activists and the Working Populace

The above trends suggest the existence of a sharp and growing division between the politically conscious minority and the passive majority in Chinese society. The first methodologically rigorous opinion survey conducted in communist China tends to confirm such a conclusion. It indicates that a high percentage of the less-educated segment of the population believes it receives equal treatment from government and can at times elicit a positive response from local government officials (despite the passivity noted above), while the better-educated are much less likely to hold such views. Equally important, this survey also indicates that, despite the increasing diversity of Chinese society, a large number of citizens express a continued intolerance of "deviant" social and political behavior.[8] This suggests that intellectual dissent and pro-democracy views enjoy little support among the broader population, including members of the rising urban middle class. Such intolerance may be especially strong in rural areas and less developed, more conservative parts of the country such as the inland provinces.

---

[7]Anita Chan, "Revolution or Corporatism? Workers and Trade Unions in Post-Mao China," *Australian Journal of Chinese Affairs,* No. 29, January 1993, pp. 52–57.

[8]This is particularly true among the lesser-educated and older groups of society. But even the better-educated are less tolerant than their counterparts in other countries. See Nathan and Shi (1993), pp. 111–116.

The gap between political activists and the masses is further aggravated by the generally elitist notion of democracy held by most political dissidents. Even the most ardent democratic intellectuals question the desirability of including ordinary citizens in the political process. The more politically conscious stratum of dissatisfied intellectuals tends to see the purpose of democracy as providing a "vital collective" opposed to corruption, nepotism, abuse of power, gerontocracy, and dogma, not the protection of individual political rights and the provision of a Western-style, competitive, majority-rule government based on the notion of "one man, one vote."[9] Understandably, working classes generally resent this condescending attitude and often do not seek input from political activists.[10]

IMPLICATIONS: A SOCIETY IN TRANSITION

The above trends and features present some closely interrelated implications for overall social stability and government policy over the next 10–15 years and beyond:

- The danger of widespread social upheaval in the event of a weakened, paralyzed government or a significant, prolonged decline in economic growth levels

- Increasing incentives for government policies keyed to further economic reform, combined with greater pressures to incorporate genuine social interests into the policy process, especially those of the urban middle class

- Possible popular support for a more assertive and chauvinistic foreign policy that seeks to utilize the greater leverage provided by China's increasing economic, diplomatic, and military clout.

---

[9]Overholt (1993), pp. 99–100.

[10]For example, the illegal Beijing Autonomous Workers' Federation formed during the Tiananmen incident of April–June 1989 was openly disrespectful of intellectual authority and very independent in its outlook and behavior. The federation did not call for an independent political party or a multi-party system in China, however. It sought only to become a voluntary institution representing a sectoral interest. See Andrew Walder and Gong Xiaoxia, "Workers in the Tiananmen Protests: The Politics of the Beijing Workers' Autonomous Federation," *Australian Journal of Chinese Affairs*, No. 29, January 1993, pp. 1–29.

Social Upheaval?

The Chinese government is sitting on a powderkeg. An explosion is by no means inevitable, however. Economic modernization and related patterns of urbanization have not yet produced cohesive and self-conscious social forces with distinct interests and demands for political involvement. Instead, a broad-based "cult" of economic progress and materialism has emerged that is less tolerant of corruption and other forms of elite malfeasance and at the same time is receptive to a strong government that can repress socially disruptive dissent. Over the long term, however, the deep-seated fears and concerns of many sectors of society about future reforms argue for the creation of a more responsive government with genuine mechanisms for mediating social conflicts and aggregating public and group attitudes.

Incorporating Social Interests

The leadership's ability to avoid a social explosion will depend greatly upon the preservation of political unity, continued successes in limiting excessive urban expansion, and, most importantly, the maintenance of moderately high economic growth rates combined with attempts to ensure adequate access by broad segments of society to the resulting benefits. The urban middle class, centered on the emerging business elite, has yet to exert much influence but will likely play an increasingly important role in this process of government adaptation to social pressures. If these efforts fail in a major way, China's social environment could become a catalyst for widespread domestic conflict.

As suggested above, such highly dynamic social conditions increase the likelihood that the military would intervene in politics to assure political order. They also strongly suggest the need for the creation of corporatist-style structures that more accurately reflect the interests of (especially economic) social groups, in order to develop a stronger sense of popular commitment to and stable involvement in the political process.

Popular Support for a More Chauvinistic Foreign Policy?

The conservative nationalist sentiments of a major portion of the Chinese populace present potentially ominous implications for Chinese foreign policy. These views suggest, for example, that many ordinary Chinese citizens believe the government should greatly accelerate its acquisition of more advanced military weaponry and adopt a more assertive diplomatic stance. These are seen in some quarters as necessary to ensure that the nation's claims to Taiwan, the Spratly Islands, and other disputed territories and boundaries are resolved in China's favor and that China is not pressured "unfairly" by other nations over a host of issues, from trade and investment to sovereignty over Tibet. Although such views have always existed to varying degrees among the Chinese public, Chinese observers insist that they have intensified greatly in recent years. Some sources even suggest that government officials (particularly moderates within the Ministry of Foreign Affairs) seek to avoid a more open and free-ranging domestic discussion of emotional subjects such as Taiwan and the Spratlys. These officials may fear that popular sentiments would be manipulated by supporters of "neo-conservatism" within the Chinese leadership (and among security specialists—see below) to strengthen their demands for a more xenophobic and chauvinistic foreign policy stance.[11]

SPECIALIST VIEWS ON CHINA'S SECURITY ENVIRONMENT

Greater access by foreigners during the reform period to Chinese intellectual circles and to a wider array of publications on strategic issues permits an assessment of broad trends in strategic thinking among specialist groups. Although largely marginal before the reforms, many of these groups today exert significant influence on the foreign policy decisionmaking process as advisors to senior leaders and providers of information and analysis to key government and party organs. In addition, the views of some groups gain significant support from important elements within both party and military leadership circles and draw upon certain public attitudes, as suggested above.

---

[11]These sentiments were conveyed to the author through personal communication with various individuals in China in the fall of 1994.

A wide reading of the available literature on security issues[12] and private discussions with Chinese specialists suggest that at least three major views toward China's current and future security environment have emerged among various groups of specialists:

- A mainstream, balance-of-power, realpolitik approach that combines suspicion of the United States with a recognition of the need for continued cooperation with the West and the maintenance of a placid regional environment

- A more conservative variant of the mainstream that stresses increased regional turbulence and uncertainty and Western hostility toward China and draws upon the above-mentioned "neo-conservative" school of thought

- A distinctly minority non-mainstream view that recognizes the growing importance of global interdependence and the consequent need to qualify or reject the realpolitik approach for a more cooperative approach to the West and more extensive participation in emerging multilateral forums.

The Mainstream Approach

This conventional view of China's security environment and its most appropriate strategy for ensuring the defense of the country is closely associated with the dominant pro-reform bureaucratic technocrats within the leadership and the mainstream foreign policy establishment. It is also most likely supported by a majority of the military elite. On the broadest level, this view seeks to balance elements of competition and cooperation with the West while maintaining both strategic independence and a strong emphasis on civilian economic development. Most importantly, it does not assume (although it may suspect) that the United States is targeting China as its primary strategic enemy. The constituent elements of this approach are presented in considerable detail in Chapter Five, in the discussion of the central principles likely to guide China's global and regional security policy during the post-Deng period.

---

[12]A secondary source of particular significance is Wang Jianwei and Lin Zhimin, "Chinese Perceptions in the Post–Cold War Era: Three Images of the United States," *Asian Survey*, Vol. 32, No. 10, October 1992, pp. 902–917.

The Conservative Variant

This variation of the mainstream approach is reportedly espoused by specialists in various party and government advisory bodies, especially those with links to major figures among China's gerontocracy. Its influence on China's political leadership is reportedly increasing, but has not (yet) eclipsed the mainstream viewpoint.

While sharing many of the central tenets of the mainstream, this view places particular emphasis on several potentially threatening and destabilizing features of China's security environment in the post–Cold War era resulting from the reemergence of old strains and rivalries, the creation of new ones, and a narrowing of the power disparities between the United States, Japan, and Europe. Hence, it argues for a likely increase in global and regional economic and political tensions over the long term. The central elements of this approach include growing concerns over the reemergence of Japan as a major military actor in the region, the reassertion of traditional Russian expansionism,[13] greater ethnic and other instabilities in Inner Asia, and, most significant, increased U.S. efforts to restrain China's economic development and attainment of great power status. In the Asia-Pacific region, such perceptions are linked to an increased likelihood of limited, local conflicts, an increased potential for the emergence of arms races, growing challenges to territory claimed by the Chinese (especially the Spratly Islands in the South China Sea), and problems over Taiwan. The latter two factors relate to the highly emotional, nationalist issues of reuniting the motherland and redressing long-standing limitations on Chinese authority in the international arena.

 One especially disturbing subvariant of this conservative viewpoint has been gaining influence since the Tiananmen incident of June 1989. Proponents argue that the United States has already become China's primary strategic enemy and will likely remain so over the long term. Supporters of this viewpoint also believe that relative declines in U.S. power and influence in Asia are producing an escalat-

---

[13]However, this point appears to generate considerable controversy among both conservatives and mainstream strategists. Some individuals apparently believe that Russian expansionism will not reemerge, if at all, for many years, given that country's enormous internal problems.

ing pattern of political and economic confrontation between the United States and its allies and friends in the region, especially Japan. Equally important, these confrontations are seen as contributing to various types of anti-U.S., exclusionist Pan-Asianist sentiments across the region (e.g., the views of Mahathir in Malaysia). As a result, advocates of this viewpoint argue that China is now confronted with a unique opportunity to greatly increase its influence in the region by positioning itself as a champion of Asian interests against the United States. To many proponents of this view, the success of such a strategy would require the formation of a Sino-Japanese alliance.[14] Not surprisingly, this viewpoint is voiced primarily by *civilian* conservative strategists. Although some military planners certainly support the notion that the United States has become China's primary strategic threat and will thus likely provoke confrontations with China over issues such as Taiwan and the Spratly Islands, few believe that an alliance with Japan is possible, or even desirable.

This conservative viewpoint thus argues that China must preserve or enhance its independent diplomatic and economic leverage, resist cooperation with the West, and focus greater attention on the development of a stronger military. Hence, it clearly shares many basic assumptions of the above-mentioned "neo-conservative" outlook evident within the military leadership and broader social circles, especially assumptions about the pernicious effect of foreign influence within China.

The Non-Mainstream, Progressive View

The third approach is generally associated with specialists within the foreign affairs and economic reform bureaucracies at the center as well as some policy institutes and economic organs outside Beijing, especially those located in the coastal areas. In addition, a relatively small number of primarily younger military officers may also sympa-

---

[14]Such an alliance is viewed as possible because of several newly emerging factors, e.g., the worsening state of U.S.-Japan relations (which they believe will eventually lead to the abrogation of the current bilateral security alliance), Tokyo's conciliatory diplomatic stance toward Beijing, growing economic interdependencies between China and Japan, China's increased economic and military capabilities (which will supposedly reduce any future concerns over the consequences of increasing Japanese power), and the common racial and cultural origins of the two Asian countries.

thize with certain tenets of this approach, as indicated in Chapter Two. This view recognizes the increasing importance of global inter-dependence in the world economy and political order. As a result, it sees the need to qualify or reject China's traditional realpolitik ap-proach to international politics in favor of greater global and regional cooperation in solving common problems associated with rapid eco-nomic, technological, and social development.

This approach thus views the United States more as a potential part-ner than an assumed rival over the long term. It asserts that Washington will increasingly need to ally with other developed states, and thus to share and coordinate power among many organi-zations, to solve the above problems. Some adherents of this ap-proach even approve of U.S. leadership in world affairs, arguing that Washington is the only power capable of organizing solutions to global problems. More specifically, in sharp contrast to the (neo-) conservative approach, some proponents believe that the United States recognizes the importance of order, prosperity, and stability in China for regional and global security and that the two countries share many common interests in maintaining regional and global stability.[15] Therefore, this approach wants China to move closer to international norms and standards, significantly modify its past rigid adherence to "strategic independence," and drop attempts to ma-nipulate or exacerbate "contradictions" among the major powers. It also opposes placing a high priority on military modernization.

IMPLICATIONS: A GROWING INTELLECTUAL FERMENT

The key features of the above approaches to China's security envi-ronment suggest several major implications for the country's future outlook toward the Asia-Pacific region:

*   The predominance of the conventional realpolitik, coopera-tive/competitive approach to China's future security in intellec-tual, specialist circles, despite considerable discussion over the global and regional changes of the past several years

---

[15]Wang and Lin (1992).

- The existence of two significant minority schools of thought that could exert greater influence over the medium to long term, with support from important institutions and groups outside the foreign-policy community

- Of the two alternatives, the hardline, "neo-conservative" variant of the conventional approach, associated with elements within the military, is more likely to gain greatly in influence

- The other alternative, non-mainstream "progressive" viewpoint offers the prospect of a fundamental transformation in China's future security stance, with decidedly positive implications for U.S. regional interests; however, this view will probably not attain a significant position of influence over Chinese security policy during the next 10–15 years.

The mainstream approach is largely congruent with China's conventional strategic outlook of the past thirty-five years. Moreover, prevailing domestic economic trends and features strongly support this viewpoint, as indicated in Chapter Four. However, the existence of both conservative and progressive undercurrents in strategic thinking suggests that China's basic foreign policy approach *might* experience significant changes in the post-Deng period. Such developments would almost certainly require the emergence of strong links between a particular intellectual, specialist viewpoint and specific policy-based leadership coalitions and military groups. For example, military conservatives might combine with hardliners within the foreign policy establishment and opponents of more radical reform within the government and party bureaucracy (and also play on popular nationalist sentiments) to greatly increase the salience of the conservative specialist approach to China's future security policy.

The non-mainstream, progressive view offers a much clearer alternative to the conventional approach and could provide the intellectual underpinnings for a radical, and positive, transformation in Chinese foreign policy, including a far more cooperative stance toward the United States. However, such a development would almost certainly face considerable opposition among both the political-military leadership and the foreign policy establishment. It could most likely take place only if a strong counteralliance to the conservatives were to emerge, including not only the above mentioned elements of the foreign policy community but also leading figures among the radical reformers, subnational political and economic elites that benefit most from external economic contacts, and progressive elements of the military. The emergence of such a counteralliance would obviously depend greatly on various future domestic political and economic developments, as well as the behavior of key foreign actors such as the United States and Japan. These factors are discussed in Chapter Five.

Chapter Four

ECONOMIC TRENDS

Since the advent of the reform period fifteen years ago, China's economy has undergone a major structural transformation. The former closed Soviet-style, planned system of the Maoist period, marked by collectivized agriculture and heavy industrial production through huge state enterprises, has been gradually replaced by a highly decentralized, relatively open, and marketized economy increasingly keyed to the manufacture of light consumer goods for foreign and domestic markets and significant inputs of foreign capital, equipment, and technology. This transformation has brought about revolutionary changes in Chinese production levels, patterns and volumes of manufacturing and trade, personal income levels, government revenues, and foreign exchange earnings that have major implications for China's future domestic stability and regional stance. Some of these changes are illustrated in Figures 4.1 through 4.3.

Six major positive and negative economic trends and features of the past decade will likely prove especially significant in the future:

- High national growth levels, through major increases in private and semi-private production, trade, and investment, largely resulting from economic reform

- Major decentralization of economic decisionmaking and the emergence of significant levels of local government and enterprise autonomy over spending and investment

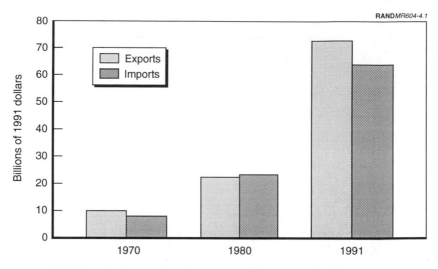

SOURCE: World Bank, *World Development Report*, 1993.

Figure 4.1—China's Merchandise Trade Growth

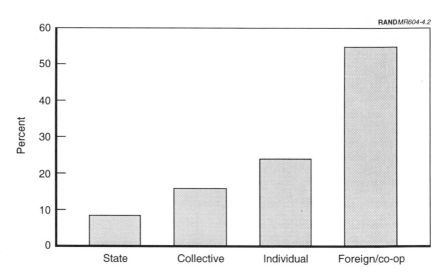

SOURCE: Overholt (1993), p. 74, derived from China State Statistical Bureau information.

Figure 4.2—Growth Rates by Type of Ownership, 1991

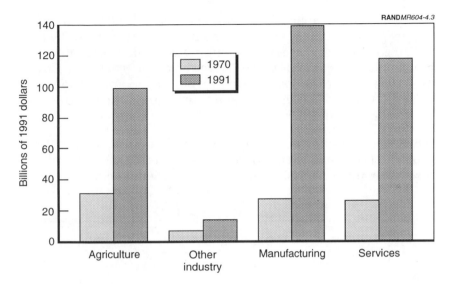

SOURCE: World Bank (1993).

Figure 4.3—China's Sectoral Growth

- Rapid increases in personal income and savings levels and provincial growth rates, leading to significant disparities across key sectors and regions

- Major decreases in state sector output and profitability and resulting declines in government revenues, combined with increasing public expenditures

- Explosive growth in foreign economic relations, leading to growing economic linkages with global and regional economies, especially in China's coastal areas.

SUSTAINED HIGH GROWTH THROUGH AN EXPANDING PRIVATE SECTOR

China has maintained "unsustainable" economic growth rates for over a decade. In 1981, Deng Xiaoping and the Chinese leadership set a goal of quadrupling GNP between 1980 and 2000.[1] This would require growth rates somewhat over 7 percent per year. At the time, such a goal was viewed as overly ambitious within China and nearly impossible by the outside world. Nevertheless, actual economic performance has well outpaced even this optimistic projection. The Chinese economy has been expanding at an annual average of more than 9 percent since 1980, as shown in Figure 4.4.[2]

While the state still plays a heavy hand in Chinese economic affairs, roughly 80 percent of commodities in China are now distributed through market channels at prices set largely by the market.[3] Five

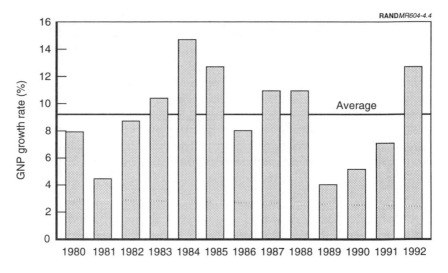

SOURCE: China State Statistical Bureau. Adapted from Overholt (1993), p. 30.

Figure 4.4—China's Economic Performance, 1980–1992

---

[1]*Mainichi Shimbun*, April 15, 1981, p. 7, reprinted in *FBIS-CHI, Daily Report—People's Republic of China*, April 16, 1991, Annex, p. 2.

[2]Also see Central Intelligence Agency, *China's Economy in 1992 and 1993, Grappling with the Risks of Rapid Growth*, Directorate of Intelligence, Washington, D.C., August 1993.

[3]Sutter et al. (1993), p. 4.

factors account for this growth and may indicate future growth prospects:

- *Capital Formation.* China has sustained high levels of savings and investment, allowing the capital stock to grow appreciably. High levels of investment can continue to produce high growth rates, but diminishing returns to investment will eventually dominate.

- *Education.* Education is highly regarded in China, and consequently investment in human capital remains high for a nation at this level of development. As with physical capital formation, the benefits from human capital formation will eventually reach diminishing returns.

- *Gains from Trade.* Chinese integration into the international economy has greatly increased productivity and efficiency within China. Such gains go beyond traditional concepts of comparative advantage. In China, opening to external economies exposed the country to advanced product standards and technologies and provided some competition to domestic producers.

- *Technology Catch-Up.* Chinese technologies lag behind world levels in most sectors of the economy. Because China can observe technological paths that have worked elsewhere, it may be able to sustain high levels of growth by implementing proven technologies.[4]

- *Economic Reform.* Chinese economic policies have been so misguided in the past that high levels of growth could be generated simply by undoing past mistakes through organizational and procedural reforms. From this point of view, China's bad policies are a valuable natural resource, but a nonrenewable one.

Of these five factors, the gains in productivity that have resulted from China's economic reforms have been the most significant. Moreover, more extensive structural reform of the economy will largely provide the key to continued high rates of growth over the

---

[4]The technology catch-up effect is by no means universally accepted, however. Some would claim that benefits accrue from remaining at the cutting edge of technologies rather than by chasing them.

medium to long term. Although the central planning process has largely been dismantled and most prices are set outside the plan, government interference in the economy remains pervasive. The Chinese fiscal system needs to be overhauled to stem a financial hemorrhage in the public sector and to make the tax and government spending systems more compatible with a market system. Remaining restrictions on international trade and an inconvertible currency still impede the formation of links (which are nonetheless extensive) with the outside world. Property and labor rights remain ill-formed or extremely restrictive. Moreover, a two-tiered pricing structure that remains in many state-dominated sectors continues to present obvious opportunities for corruption, many of which are being exploited at an accelerating rate. Finally, energy prices and production remain largely controlled, creating notable shortages.

Many of these and other problems seen in the Chinese economy result from the transition from a planned economy to a market economy. Their alleviation or elimination requires the successful completion of a higher stage of reform, designed to maximize the free flow of money, goods, human capital, and property. Yet steady progress toward this goal is by no means assured. It will likely require a level of expertise, political will, and ideological flexibility that may not exist within the Chinese leadership.

DECENTRALIZATION OF ECONOMIC DECISIONMAKING

The transformation of China from a centrally planned statist economy to a largely market-driven economy has drastically decentralized economic decisionmaking, thus fundamentally altering the nature of center-local and interregional economic relations. This process consists of several major developments, including (a) an explosion in the number of subnational economic decisionmaking units,[5] (b) the transfer of many government functions and re-

---

[5]The most significant decisionmaking units created under the reforms include: 7 economic regions, over 100 interprovincial and interregional organizations of economic cooperation, 4 special economic zones (SEZs), 14 coastal open cities, nine core cities with quasi-provincial-level economic authority, 27 high-technology zones with SEZ-style policies and privileges, nearly 170 major cities controlling over 700 satellite counties, 480,000 semi-private or private enterprises, and millions of small collective enterprises.

sources[6] downward and outward, and (c) a major increase in the use of informal over formal mechanisms and relationships to conduct economic transactions.[7]

These trends have produced several consequences. While the central government retains major (primarily indirect) controls over the Chinese economy in critical areas such as top-level personnel selection, legislation and regulation, information dissemination, and administrative skills, it possesses far fewer direct economic resources and means for compliance than in the past. In contrast, both provinces and municipalities show a greater ability to assert their economic interests[8] and increasingly seek to deflect the intent of major central economic reforms such as fiscal recentralization and increased enterprise autonomy.[9]

However, Beijing has not lost economic controls uniformly throughout China. Rather, it has selectively liberalized economic policies in a growing network of special economic zones, major municipalities, and investment areas. China's coastal areas in particular enjoy the greatest degree of local autonomy at present. Such areas have clearly benefitted the most from the overall decentralization of economic authority under the reforms, as well as the specific privileges extended as part of the "open door" policy, including the establishment of coastal special economic zones and investment areas and the de-

---

[6]These include, most notably, control over formal legislative rules and procedures, the executive authority to undertake major economic decisions in such areas as investment, taxation, production, and trade, and the selection of key economic and administrative personnel in bureaus and enterprises.

[7]Such informal procedures include unsanctioned and often illegal interactions between individuals. This has led to a significant increase in the level of economic corruption in China.

[8]For example, the most advanced provinces and municipalities enjoy greatly expanded financial powers, unprecedented autonomy in price reform, the ability to levy new local taxes and fees, greater freedom in selecting personnel below the level of provincial vice governor, much greater managerial power over state and nonstate enterprises, and expanded controls over local investment decisions and foreign trade activities.

[9]This is done, for example, through the creative interpretation or flexible implementation of central policies and measures. For more on this and other points above, see Barry Naughton, "Hierarchy and the Bargaining Economy: Government and Enterprise in the Reform Process," in Kenneth G. Lieberthal and Michael Lampton (eds.), *Bureaucracy, Politics, and Decision Making in Post-Mao China*, University of California Press, Berkeley, 1992, pp. 245–279.

centralization of China's foreign trade system. But a growing tendency toward urban-centered regionalization suggests that major municipalities throughout the coastal areas are enjoying increasing levels of influence over economic development patterns. This trend could become predominant over the medium and long term.

Overall, the decentralization of economic decisionmaking authority has led to the emergence in China of a far more complex economic system, characterized by pervasive bargaining over all essential transactions (e.g., price, plan, supply, tax, and credit), much higher levels of corruption, greatly enhanced local government control over enterprises, and a relatively weaker center.

DISPARITIES IN INCOMES AND PROVINCIAL/REGIONAL GROWTH RATES

A tightly controlled statist economy can be very effective in maintaining rough equality of income across regions, albeit at a very low level. The Chinese government, since the early 1980s, has backed away from notions of equality of economic outcomes as it has embraced economic reform. Liberalizing the economy has permitted— and thus, definitionally, exacerbated—large inequalities in income. Indeed, the gap between urban and rural living standards is much wider in China than elsewhere in Northeast Asia.[10] Moreover, one would expect some regions to prosper and others to languish under a market economy. In China, these regional inequalities have been exaggerated, unintentionally, through the implementation of reforms. Those coastal areas that have historically been more prosperous were allowed (with the exception of Shanghai) to implement economic reforms earliest. The results are hardly surprising: Income levels in the southern coastal provinces generally outstrip those of inland provinces.

In the past, the inland areas had depended considerably on the central government to redress some of these differences. The capacity of

---

[10]Nicholas R. Lardy, *China in the World Economy*, Institute for International Economics, Washington, 1994. Lardy states that ". . . China's overall income inequality exceeds that in Taiwan and South Korea and is comparable to that observed in several South and Southeast Asian countries" (p. 24).

the central government to perform this role in the future is, as described below, much in doubt. However, the share of China's total population living in absolute poverty has declined greatly under the reforms, from about one-third in the late seventies to less than a tenth by the mid eighties, thus reducing pressures upon the central government to alleviate intense poverty.[11] Moreover, all regions of the nation have gained economically from the reforms (see Figures 4.5 and 4.6). Those provinces with the lowest growth rates are doing poorly only by Chinese standards. Thus, so long as economic growth continues at a moderately rapid yet uneven pace, the need for centrally directed redistribution may be low. However, a prolonged and major economic slowdown, particularly one that froze the current disparities into place, would likely create internal political problems for the Chinese government. On the other hand, an excessively rapid, prolonged pace of economic growth (e.g., 10 percent or more annual increases) could greatly exacerbate the existing social and political tensions discussed in Chapters Two and Three.

DECLINING FISCAL CAPACITY OF CENTRAL AND LOCAL GOVERNMENTS

As markets replace planning, control of financial levers becomes increasingly important. The past decade was marked by a steady transfer from Beijing to the provinces of many key financial levers, accompanied by a delegation to local governments of responsibility for tax administration. Today, China as a whole, but particularly the central government, is facing a severe fiscal crunch. This crunch is, again, an unintended consequence of economic reform. Figure 4.7 shows the decline in central government revenues both as a share of GNP and as a share of overall government expenditures.

Although fiscal problems are most severe at the central government level, all levels of government are experiencing fiscal difficulties. In many cases, revenues are actually growing but they still lag behind economic growth and public expenditure needs.

---

[11]Lardy (1994), p. 20.

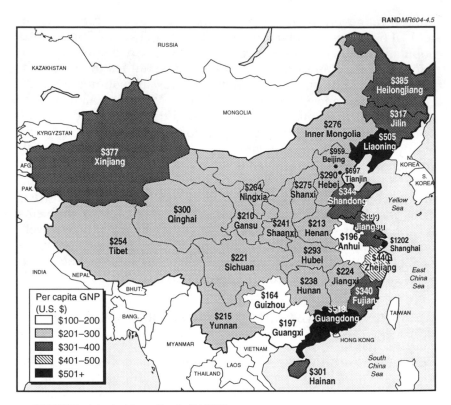

SOURCE: Adapted from Overholt (1993).

Figure 4.5—Per Capita GNP, 1991

Historically, the People's Republic of China has raised much of its public funds through earnings of state enterprises. The central government was also able to direct resources at favorable prices through the planning process. Economic reform has reduced the relative importance of state enterprises in the economy as the private and small-scale collective sectors have grown and competition from more efficient enterprises has cut into the earnings of state enterprises. The ability of the state to control resources and prices has been severely curtailed—the sine qua non of reform.

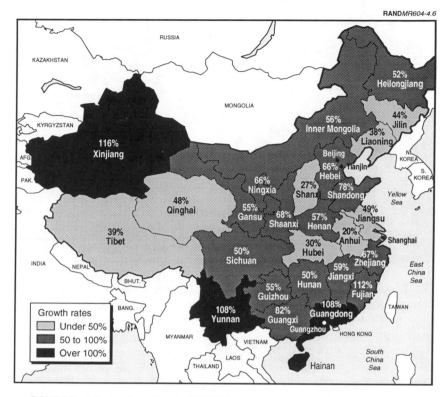

SOURCE: Adapted from Overholt (1993).

Figure 4.6—Real Income Growth by Province, 1985–1991

While traditional sources of revenue have thus shrunk drastically, the Chinese state has yet to effectively raise revenue from the growing private and collective sectors. Although central government expenditures have continued to grow, they have not kept pace with GNP growth. During the 1980s, economic growth of almost 9 percent was accompanied by central government expenditures growing at about 3.5 percent, according to U.S. government sources.[12] Tax

---

[12]U.S. Arms Control and Disarmament Agency (1990).

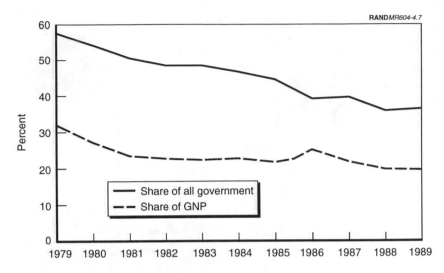

SOURCES: Jia Hao and Lin Zhimin (eds.), *Changing Central-Local Relations in China, Reform and State Capacity*, Westview Press, Boulder, Colorado, 1994, p. 99; U.S. Arms Control and Disarmament Agency, *World Military Expenditures and Arms Transfers*, 1990.

Figure 4.7— China's Fiscal Problems

reforms enacted in 1994, including the announcement of a value-added tax (VAT), may indicate progress, but it remains to be seen whether the central government will efficiently tap the resources of private and collective enterprises, where most revenues are being generated.[13] Under the new reforms, the government devised a tax assignment system intended to increase the central-local tax revenue ratio from 40:60 to 60:40; however, no deadline has been set for realizing this goal. Also problematic is the means of tax collection. China's taxing bureaucracy has been under provincial and local control, but the 1994 reforms included measures for the establishment at

---

[13]Primary examples of the latter are the locally run township and village enterprises, which have generated most of the productive wealth under the reforms.

the local levels of a tax collection system for the central government. It is unclear how successful these new measures will be.[14]

Compounding the revenue problems is a need for greater public spending. The economic reforms are eroding the long-standing links between worker and enterprise. In the past, while the economy was largely statist, many of the social services normally provided by governments in market economies were performed by enterprises. Enterprises would provide health care, housing, rations of food, retirement, and rough analogs of unemployment insurance and disability insurance. Enterprises could not fail, and workers had great difficulty changing jobs. Economic reforms have partially liberalized the labor market, and private and collective enterprises can now fail, at least in theory. A set of government-funded social programs—a social "safety net"—thus needs to replace the services traditionally performed by enterprises. Other pressing needs for public expenditure include:

- Addressing major infrastructure, energy, and environmental problems and general bottlenecks generated by rapid growth

- Alleviating socioeconomic disparities across provinces and regions

- Modernizing military capabilities

- Constraining population growth and excessive population movements.

The success of the economic reforms has therefore trapped the Chinese government between declining revenues and growing demands for public spending. The fiscal crunch will affect both the central government and the provinces, but is likely to be particularly severe for the central government, which remains dependent on provincial and local tax collectors. This fiscal crunch further strengthens the provincial and local governments relative to the central government.

---

[14] Tsang Shu-ki and Cheng Yuk-shing, "China's Tax Reforms of 1994: Breakthrough or Compromise?" *Asian Survey*, Vol. 34, No. 9, September 1994, pp. 769–788.

GROWING ECONOMIC INTERACTION WITH THE OUTSIDE

The Chinese economic reforms owe a great measure of their success to an opening of China to the outside world. On the eve of the reform period, in 1977, China's total trade was less than $15 billion and it ranked 30th as an exporting country. By 1993, China's total trade had approached $200 billion, accounting for 2.2 percent of world trade, and it had become the world's 10th largest exporting country. China has also become a significant recipient of foreign aid and a major borrower on international capital markets and is attracting significant amounts of foreign investment. Approved foreign investment in 1993 exceeded $110 billion, almost double the 1992 level.[15]

There are two aspects to this opening. First, the general liberalization of trade and investment has provided raw materials, intermediate goods, technology, capital, and markets for the Chinese manufacturing sector. Foreign trade and investment have allowed Chinese enterprises to prosper even when domestic markets for their inputs and products are poorly formed, distorted by remaining controls, or nonexistent. Second, the opening has allowed the growth of significant economic ties with advanced capitalist countries, especially the United States and Japan. For example, during the reform period, U.S. imports from China have risen from approximately $300 million to $26 billion and exports to China have grown from about $800 million to nearly $7.5 billion. The value of U.S. direct investment contracts with China has also risen significantly under the reforms, from approximately $470 million in 1983 to more than $3 billion in 1992, with major increases in recent years.[16]

Japanese trade with and investment in China have not shown such dramatic increases over the entire reform period. However, this is now beginning to change dramatically. Japan's exports to China almost doubled between 1990 and 1992 and continue to rise sharply. Japanese imports from China have also shown very significant, albeit

---

[15]See Lardy (1994), pp. 2–3.

[16]Lardy (1994), pp. 34, 74, 118–119. Actual investment levels are significantly less than contracted levels but have also shown significant increases in recent years.

somewhat lesser, increases.[17] Moreover, Japanese companies have recently surpassed U.S. firms as a source of actual (not contracted) foreign direct investment in China.[18] Finally, Japanese development assistance has been especially important to China during the reform period. Throughout the eighties, Japan on average supplied more than three-quarters of all the official development loans received by China and has been by far the largest single source of grant funds.[19]

Of even greater importance than China's links with major industrialized economies are the fast-growing regional ties between coastal China, Hong Kong, and Taiwan. Although largely informal, these ties have fostered an expanding network of trade and investment relations among the three areas, resulting in the formation of a "Greater China" economic subregion. Additional economic ties with South Korea and Singapore are also forming. This highly dynamic process is largely beyond the control of China's central government.

The development of "Greater China" can be seen in trade statistics. Between 1980 and 1991, exports from Hong Kong to China grew at 31 percent while imports grew at 24 percent. Taiwan's total exports and imports grew at 12 and 11 percent, respectively. Exports to and imports from China grew at 27 and 24 percent. This occurred in the face of continuing prohibitions on direct trade with Taiwan. In south China, the links are even more significant. In 1991, 85 percent of Guangdong's exports and 74 percent of its imports flowed through Hong Kong. For Fujian, these figures were 37 and 53 percent.[20] The role of foreign direct investment (FDI) in regional trade is also significant. Forty percent of Guangdong's exports were from FDI ventures in 1991. Similarly in Fujian, 43 percent of exports were from FDI

---

[17]Today Japan exports significantly more to China than the United States does, while U.S. imports from China remain greatly ahead of Japanese imports.

[18]Lardy (1994), pp. 124–125.

[19]Japan has extended three major assistance packages to China with loans totalling more than $10 billion. By the end of 1993, actual contracts signed for specific projects using these loan guarantees totalled about $5 billion. These projects are concentrated in vital infrastructure projects in the telecommunications, transportation, and energy sectors. See Lardy (1994), pp. 56, 120.

[20]Trade figures used in this paragraph were extracted from Robert F. Ash and Y. Y. Kueh, "Economic Integration Within Greater China: Trade and Investment Flows Between China, Hong Kong, and Taiwan," *China Quarterly*, No. 136, December 1993.

ventures.[21] The links within this region have allowed China to acquire capital, management, and marketing expertise from Hong Kong and Taiwan while providing low labor costs in return.

The vast majority of China's foreign investment and a large proportion of China's foreign trade activities are centered in the coastal areas. With growing ties to nearby economic dynamos such as Hong Kong, Taiwan, and South Korea, these wealthier regions face the prospect of developing into quasi-independent enclaves distinct from both China's lesser developed interior provinces and the more centrally dominated area around Beijing.

IMPLICATIONS: A RAPIDLY CHANGING ECONOMIC ENVIRONMENT

The above economic trends and features suggest major changes in the composition, geographical focus, and pattern of control over economic development that have major direct and indirect implications for China's future domestic stability and external behavior. Five implications are especially important:

- Deep-rooted structural incentives for further reform, combined with major obstacles to successful completion of its final stages

- Increased potential for internal regional tensions, kept in check by continued growth

- Possible constraints on long-term government financing of high levels of defense modernization

- Growing Chinese dependence on foreign economic relations for continued domestic growth and social stability

- A larger role for economics in determining cooperative or conflictual relations with nearby Asian nations.

---

[21]Ash and Kueh (1993).

Incentives for Further Reform, with Growing Obstacles

Since the legitimacy of the Chinese regime has become closely intertwined with Chinese economic performance, it will likely prove very difficult for Beijing to reverse or even slow the pace of economic reform. Provinces not yet granted "special" economic privileges are likely to clamor for them, and the demonstrated benefits of reform for average citizens make its further spread highly likely.

However, as reform spreads geographically and sectorally in China, the problems that have arisen already are likely to grow worse. Specifically, the fiscal "crunch" faced by central and local governments is likely to worsen, thereby preventing any resolution of the social and political tensions and dislocations created by an expanding market. Moreover, China's past cycles of rapid expansion, overheating, and inflation, followed by the often crude application of adminstrative "clampdowns" on capital construction, borrowing, and investment, could intensify, thus obstructing the creation of a more stable pattern of growth.[22]

To overcome these and other basic problems, China's leadership will be increasingly driven to implement more challenging structural reforms, designed to improve efficiency, strengthen individual incentives, foster genuine competition, and create the basis for a more unified national market. These include thoroughgoing price, tax, fiscal, and legal reforms, the further liberalization of trade and currency convertibility, and the establishment of extensive factor mobility for property, labor, and capital. Fundamental reforms of the fiscal and tax systems in particular can establish a financially strong and effective central government and a more integrated economy, essential to the ultimate success of those reforms.

Yet many of these advances will most likely produce additional social problems, with adverse political implications. For example, thoroughgoing and sudden price reform could lead to intolerable levels of inflation and urban unrest; genuine enterprise competition will greatly exacerbate worker insecurity; and the introduction of rela-

---

[22]For a recent discussion of this cycle, in the context of currently high nationwide inflation rates, see Kathy Chen and Joseph Kahn, "Nervous Beijing Backtracks on Speedy Economic Reform," *Asian Wall Street Journal*, April 7–8, 1995.

tively free markets for production factors will likely lead to the loss of state control.[23] Moreover, provincial and municipal governments have both the incentive and the ability to resist any far-reaching marketization efforts that threaten to undermine their expanded controls over economic (and especially enterprise) behavior.

The best way to avoid or alleviate many of these difficulties is to gradually implement a genuine program of political reform aimed at expanding real participation in key policy decisions by those social groups that would presumably be hardest hit by the above changes. Yet, such revolutionary actions are highly resisted by the communist leadership.

Increased Potential for Domestic Regional Tensions

Prevailing regional economic trends, when combined with the changes in provincial and central leadership discussed in Chapter One, suggest the existence of three distinct political-economic regions in China:

- A strongly pro-reform, increasingly rich, and quasi-autonomous south, weakly represented in Beijing but enjoying growing ties to the outside, especially as part of "Greater China"

- A more conservative but highly reform-oriented east and northeast, enjoying strong political representation in Beijing, but also subject to closer control by the center, with rising incomes and a diversity of domestic and foreign economic ties

- A lesser developed, highly conservative central and inland area, experiencing limited yet growing benefits from the reforms and the open-door policies, declining representation at the center, and a continued dependence on assistance from Beijing.

As noted above, Beijing's declining financial fortunes and the increased demands on central revenues *might* serve to weaken drastically the central government's redistributive capacities. This could greatly aggravate relations between the impoverished central and

---

[23]Harry Harding, *China's Second Revolution: Reform After Mao*, The Brookings Institution, Washington, D.C., 1987, Chapter 10, pp. 271–286.

inland areas and the more advanced coastal areas of the south, east, and northeast. However, declining government capabilities will probably not exacerbate provincial relations and threaten overall social stability *as long as economic development continues nation-wide.* This is because the potentially destabilizing effect of inter-provincial income disparities is greatly mitigated by the generally rapid growth rates experienced by inland areas under the reforms[24] and the fact that coastal and inland areas are becoming more eco-nomically interdependent. The latter phenomenon is reflected in increasingly positive correlations between growth rates in Guang-dong and those in nearby Sichuan and Hunan, significant increases in interprovincial capital and labor flows, increases in the amount of interior products purchased by the coastal areas, and the increasing level of remittances received from inland workers working in coastal areas.[25] Because of these most recent trends, interior provinces have begun to recognize the value of the reforms and are now pushing to obtain the same economic liberalization privileges of the coastal areas, rather than to oppose them, as in the past, by advocating greater central direction over the economy.[26]

A greater potential for tension lies between the center and the dy-namic southern coastal areas, exacerbated by the latter's very low political representation in central party and state organs, noted in Chapter Two. Thus far, these two forces have coexisted in relative harmony, largely because of the mutual benefits provided by contin-ued high rates of growth and the strong desire of the provinces to avoid challenging Beijing's authority in key areas, such as internal

---

[24]For example, relatively poor inland provinces such as Xinjiang, Qinghai, and Yunnan have experienced very high growth rates under the reforms, while the rela-tively rich coastal area of Shanghai and its environs experienced the slowest growth before 1992. See Overholt (1993), p. 98.

[25]Overholt goes so far as to state that the image of a rapidly growing coast alongside a stagnating interior is a myth (pp. 104–108). Lardy (1994) also argues that economic re-form has increased, rather than decreased, the level of economic integration between coastal and inland provinces, thus reducing pressures toward regional economic or political separatism (pp. 26–27).

[26]Overholt states (p. 102) that managers of heavy industrial state enterprises located in the interior may still suffer greatly as a result of the reforms and thus support efforts to curtail them and to strengthen central administrative controls. However, he be-lieves that any political influence wielded by such individuals is vitiated by their wide geographic dispersion, internal fragmentation, and desperate search for links with coastal or foreign firms. See p. 110.

security and foreign policy. However, such harmony could erode significantly in the future in the face of growing fiscal problems at the center and the continued exclusion of key southern elites from national political and economic decisions.

Increasing Constraints on Defense Modernization Efforts?

The Chinese military is undergoing an extensive modernization. Defense spending has been increasing steadily since the late eighties (averaging well over 10 percent per annum since 1989) and reports suggest that the Chinese leadership intends to maintain such increases for at least the remainder of the nineties, to (a) improve defense production facilities, (b) procure foreign weaponry, (c) improve internal security capabilities, (d) strengthen R&D and military engineering capabilities, and generally create a more modern force structure on a par with the industrialized West.[27]

However, the growing fiscal constraints on the central government outlined above could make financing such modernization problematic over the long term. The central government could opt to maintain (or increase) high levels of defense spending, despite such constraints, but this would likely reduce funds available to meet other critical needs, thus causing significant difficulties. For example, spending less on social programs and infrastructure investment might exacerbate domestic social and regional tensions and slow

---

[27]The Chinese defense budget increased approximately 13 percent in 1989, 15.5 percent in 1990, 12 percent in 1991, 13.8 percent in 1992, and 14.9 percent in 1993. See Chong-Pin Lin, "The People's Liberation Army and the Fourteenth Party Congress of the Chinese Communist Party," paper presented at the Fourth Annual Staunton Hill Conference on the People's Liberation Army, August 27–29, 1993. In 1994, China's defense budget increased by over 20 percent, to nearly $7 billion. It should be noted that these figures are based upon official Chinese sources, which seriously underestimate total military spending levels. Additional revenues derived from special extrabudgetary State Council appropriations, income received from China's growing number of military enterprises, and additional subsidies and activities together suggest that actual military spending levels are at least two to three times higher than official levels, and perhaps as much as six times higher. However, such increases should be significantly discounted for inflation, which has been running at approximately 20 percent for several years and is likely to increase. For further details on problems associated with the measurement of Chinese military spending, see Swaine et al. (forthcoming). For reference to future Chinese spending levels, see *South China Morning Post*, March 7, 1991, p. 1.

growth.   The likelihood of domestic unrest increases with such choices. Alternatively, the government could permit (or be forced to accept) much higher levels of military involvement in profit-making activities, which could exacerbate leadership tensions, as noted above.

On the other hand, because a significant portion of the constraints on major military modernization efforts are financial, a solution to China's fiscal problems would likely permit accelerated military modernization. The potential of China to field increasingly capable forces is, absent fiscal limitations, greatly increased by the ongoing economic modernization. A constant defense share of GNP would assure close to 10 percent per year growth in defense spending. The level of technology in the civilian economy is rising, providing a better technological base for the military sector and providing greater exposure in the population to technologies incorporated into modern weapons. Moreover, many civilian assets provide services potentially valuable to the military such as airlift, sealift, and communications.

Growing Dependence on the Global Economy

Unquestionably, China's open-door policy has produced substantial economic benefits. Before economic reform, China was largely closed to trade and could be little influenced by its external economic relations. The Chinese economy is now heavily dependent on external trade, finance, and technology, especially from the industrialized West and Japan. This dependence constrains the Chinese government from reversing the open-door policy without dire consequences and also makes China vulnerable to external economic pressure.

Much of Chinese coastal manufacturing depends critically on continued links to the outside world. In many cases, the Chinese provide labor to fabricate products from imported material using imported machinery and working for foreign management. In other nations, local supplier networks would be used to support these industries. For a number of reasons including inadequate technology and quality, poor transportation networks, poorly developed markets for intermediate goods, and inflexibility of many state enterprises, many export-oriented manufacturing firms buy little from other

Chinese firms. This is true even when other Chinese firms produce high-quality substitutes for the imported materials. Similarly, many enterprises depend almost entirely on foreign markets for their products rather than selling into the potentially large domestic market.

Over time, local supplier networks and product markets are likely to lessen China's vulnerability to outside economic pressure, and increasingly, China will have the economic stature to exert pressure of its own, again reducing its vulnerability. However, such changes will likely occur very gradually, over a relatively long period of time, and will probably not affect the general trend toward a growing level of integration between the Chinese domestic, regional, and global economies. Coping with the increasingly complex challenges posed by such integration will become a central task of China's future leadership.

Increased Influence of Economic Forces over Regional Relationships

Rapidly increasing levels of economic integration between the dynamic coastal areas and key regional economies in Taiwan, Hong Kong, South Korea, and Japan hold particularly significant implications for China's external relations. This process is creating the potential for either greater economic conflict or closer cooperation with nearby Asian nations.

The formation of an informal "Greater China" economic area addresses one aspect of the Taiwan issue. While political differences between Taiwan and China remain and continue to manifest themselves in military and diplomatic rivalry, economic ties between Taiwan and China, particularly coastal China, are growing rapidly. At a broad level, such ties can reduce tensions between China and Taiwan as each realizes its own interests in continued economic cooperation. There is some political danger if economic ties bind south China closer to Taiwan than to the rest of China: Conservatives in the central government or in inland areas may see an attempt by Taiwan to carve out a sphere of influence in south China.

Over the longer term, the most important economic relationship in the region is that between China and Japan. Even U.S. interests may be more affected by this relationship than by the bilateral relationships between the United States and these two nations. These nations are historical rivals if not enemies, but both seem unsure of how to view their economic ties. Were these two nations to cooperate economically, Japanese technology and Chinese labor, resources, and markets could prove an extremely powerful combination. Cooperation between these nations could facilitate the formation of an Asian economic area that largely excluded, intentionally or unintentionally, U.S. trade and investment. Conversely, economic conflict between China and Japan (such as both nations' pursuing neo-mercantilist policies and both attempting to dominate trade and investment elsewhere in Asia) could make U.S- Japan economic rivalry appear trivial. While conflict between China and Japan would probably assure the United States continued economic access to Asia, such an antagonistic relationship might cause destabilization in other spheres.[28]

---

[28]The Sino-Japanese economic relationship and its implications are examined in greater detail in Swaine et al. (forthcoming).

Chapter Five

IMPLICATIONS FOR CHINESE FOREIGN POLICY

The above political, social, and economic trends and features present the following general implications for China's current and future foreign policy stance over the next 10–15 years:

- China's primary foreign policy objectives support the maintenance of stable but high growth rates through a deepening of market-led, outward-oriented economic reform; this reflects a fundamental reordering of traditional foreign policy priorities.

- Secondary and tertiary foreign policy objectives include the defense of national sovereignty and unity and the attainment of big-power status; both goals are deeply rooted in growing nationalist attitudes, primarily associated with the military and conservative civilian elites.

- The above three foreign policy objectives indicate that Chinese security strategy will probably exhibit significant continuity in eight major areas, suggesting, on balance, a basis for future caution and pragmatism in China's dealings with the West.

- Such policy continuity, as well as several possible types of discontinuities, might also produce Chinese behavior and views that present various adverse consequences for U.S. regional interests; however, the potential also exists for a major discontinuity that would prove very beneficial to U.S. interests.

- The most serious adverse Chinese behavior toward the region would likely result from various forms of disruptive military intervention in leadership politics and foreign policy, probably associated with conservative nationalist sentiments and precipitated by either economic problems associated with the failure to complete more advanced stages of reform, or prolonged leadership strife arising from the succession struggle following the death of Deng Xiaoping.

PRIMARY OBJECTIVE: PRIORITY ON CONTINUED DOMESTIC REFORM

A continued stress on high growth rates through a deepening of market-led, outward-oriented economic reform will likely remain the essential goal of Chinese domestic policy over the next 10–15 years, for at least six basic reasons:

1. To strengthen incentives for cooperation among the emerging pro-reform bureaucratic-technocratic elite

2. To convince the military and conservatives among the political leadership that reform through further marketization and privatization is the only credible path to national revitalization and defense modernization

3. To fund the infrastructure, the army, and the government apparatus

4. To expand the base of support for the regime among those broad urban and rural working classes primarily concerned with income and growth, including the middle class

5. To show intellectuals and students that the regime is worth supporting, despite its authoritarian features, and to suggest that pressures for rapid democratization could threaten existing gains

6. To give the regime the ability to repress whatever opposition to reform remains among old radicals and fearful state enterprise managers and workers.[1]

---

[1]Many of these points accord with those of Overholt (1993), pp. 87–88. Overholt states that the ability of middle-ranking party and government bureaucrats to undermine the reforms is highly limited by the strength of the pro-reform leadership coalition, the pressures of a pro-reform society, and, most importantly, the fact that their families have become completely immersed in the reforms (pp. 115–116).

Such imperatives, combined with the mainstream specialist viewpoint that conflict among the major powers will remain highly unlikely for many years, have served to fundamentally reorder the priorities guiding China's external policies, including its stance toward Asia. During the pre-reform period, civilian economic development was viewed as an essentially separate, domestic issue, associated with internal aspects of mass mobilization, collectivization, and social transformation. In the context of the Cold War and growing tensions with the Soviet Union, defense of national sovereignty and the attainment of big-power status largely dominated Chinese strategic thinking. Today, however, the creation or maintenance of external conditions favoring the furtherance of reform-based civilian economic development has become the dominant motivating goal behind China's security strategy. Indeed, the Chinese leadership (and many ordinary citizens) recognize that civilian economic growth and China's external relations and future security are now inextricably linked. Thus, many Chinese believe that the economic arena will constitute the main domain of international competition in the future.[2]

SECONDARY OBJECTIVES: DEFENSE OF NATIONAL SOVEREIGNTY AND ATTAINMENT OF MAJOR-POWER STATUS[3]

Despite being relegated to secondary and tertiary levels in China's foreign policy calculus, the twin traditional goals of Chinese security policy will continue to exert enormous influence over strategic thinking. This is strongly indicated by the characteristics of China's political-military leadership, as well as the intellectual approaches to China's future strategic environment, noted above. While some radical reformers and business elites may regard economic development as primarily intended to create a prosperous and stable soci-

---

[2]For an extended defense of this last point, see David M. Lampton, "China and the Strategic Quadrangle: Foreign Policy Continuity in an Age of Discontinuity," in Michael Mandelbaum (ed.), *The Strategic Quadrangle: Japan, China, Russia, and the United States in East Asia,* Council on Foreign Relations Press, New York, 1994.

[3]For confirmation of this prioritization of China's basic strategic objectives, see Pan Shiying, *Reflections on Modern Strategy: Post Cold War Strategic Theory,* Shijie Zhishi Chubanshe, Beijing, 1993.

ety, other leadership groups, especially among the military and more conservative elements of the party and state bureaucracy, almost certainly view it as critical to the attainment of China's national defense and great-power aspirations. This latter view is also shared by intellectual supporters of the mainstream approach to the external security environment, especially its more conservative variant. These views draw upon strong emotions, linked to nationalist sentiments, traditional cultural ethnocentrism, and a deeply rooted historical sense of injustice at the hands of foreign (especially Western) countries.

LIKELY OUTCOME: CONTINUITY IN THE BASIC TENETS OF FOREIGN AND SECURITY POLICY

The above three basic priorities guiding China's foreign security policy, and their underlying political-military, social, and economic trends and features, together suggest a basis for the continued implementation of eight central tenets of China's current global and regional policy. Some of these tenets were in effect before the reforms. However, most were enunciated in various forms beginning at the Twelfth Party Congress of 1982 and have been under implementation since at least 1988.[4]

1. *Maintenance of a peaceful regional and global environment conducive to the successful implementation of domestic economic reform and defense modernization.*

This tenet is obviously most directly associated with the first basic priority of Chinese security policy (economic development) and is central to the mainstream intellectual view of China's security environment. It has been pivotal to Chinese foreign policy under the reforms. It is to be achieved through continuing the open-door policy in foreign economic relations, expanding economic and diplomatic ties with all Asian states (especially Japan), lowering the probability of armed conflict, and maintaining reasonably good relations with the United States, Europe, and Russia. This tenet also incorporates a recognition of the importance of a *comprehensive* security strategy

---

[4]Lampton (1994).

that includes political and economic means, not just military power, and a basic belief that China faces no pressing external military threat. The United States is seen to desire continued positive relations with China, for a variety of primarily economic and geopolitical reasons, while Russia is expected to experience economic weakness and political disorder for many more years.[5] Finally, this tenet also involves significant but *limited* Chinese support for multilateral initiatives, U.N. peacekeeping efforts, and other regional activities intended to promote more cooperative patterns of behavior in the region.

Maintaining reasonably good relations with the United States is seen as particularly essential for several reasons:

- To assure the continued success of China's economic reform program, through Western trade, technology, and investment

- To avoid excessive external pressures on China's military modernization program

- To counter the possible emergence of a more economically or militarily assertive Japan

- To lower, to the extent possible, U.S. incentives for providing military assistance to Taiwan

- To resolve critical issues of mutual concern such as the acquisition of nuclear weapons by Korea or Japan and the possible long-term reemergence of an expansionist Russia.

2. *Reliance on the modalities of realpolitik, balance-of-power politics, and an avoidance of entangling alliances.*

This tenet has been fundamental to Chinese security strategy since at least the beginning of the Sino-Soviet split in the late fifties. Sustained by a Chinese sense of vulnerability in a fluid geopolitical environment, it stresses the search for strategic leverage and independence of action through the balancing and manipulation of eco-

---

[5]Lampton (1994).

nomic,[6] diplomatic, and military relations among both major and emerging powers. Among the former countries, such Chinese actions are often designed to weaken, break up, or prevent the emergence of a dominant power or an alignment of powers opposed to China.

During the Cold War, this tenet found its clearest expression in the strategic triangle comprising the United States, China, and the Soviet Union. Since the end of the Cold War, it is reflected in a more complex set of Chinese interactions with a variety of powers, including the United States, Japan, the Association of Southeast Asian Nations (ASEAN), and, to a lesser extent, key West European countries such as Germany. In this new environment, the United States is viewed with particular suspicion as the only remaining superpower in a multipolar world, increasingly challenged by emerging major powers such as Germany and Japan, constrained by its internal economic and political weaknesses, critical to Chinese development, yet seeking to prevent China's full emergence as a major economic and military power.[7] Japan is seen as both a key source of economic assistance and political leverage in dealing with Washington (given the many problems facing the U.S.-Japan relationship) and probably China's primary potential foe over the long term. Despite Tokyo's protestations to the contrary, many Chinese defense planners in particular remain concerned that Japan will eventually translate its enormous and growing economic power in Asia into significant political and perhaps military influence, thus posing a major challenge to China's strategic position in the region. On the other hand, Japan is also viewed as a key source of economic, financial, and technological assistance.

---

[6]In recent years, this tenet has placed an increasing emphasis on the use of economic appeals to build international support for Chinese objectives and to make major powers aware that opposing core Chinese interests will likely undermine their own economic interests. This point is stressed by Lampton (1994).

[7]As a result of such complexities, this tenet contains important differences over how long U.S. dominance in the post–Cold War era will last and what the ultimate effect of that dominance will be. As suggested in previous chapters, some Chinese strategists believe such dominance will lead to greater U.S. cooperation with Germany and Japan; others argue that the United States will be driven by intensifying economic competition to contend with both countries and eventually seek dominance over them.

From the Chinese perspective, these critical features have led to the emergence of a geopolitical and geoeconomic triangle in Asia between China, Japan, and the United States, albeit with additional complications presented by the emergence of secondary players such as India, South Korea, Taiwan, and many of the ASEAN states. This new triangle is viewed as providing China with numerous opportunities to improve its strategic position in relation to its most critical protagonists.[8]

Chinese behavior in such a complex strategic environment is characterized by a flexible, sometimes conciliatory, and often expedient diplomatic approach. Central elements include:

- The search for closer political and economic relations with potential rivals of the United States, such as Japan, Russia, and Germany

- The development of common interests with most Third World (and especially Asian) states, to raise China's global stature and increase Beijing's bargaining leverage with the United States and Japan, especially on important economic and political issues

- Increased, albeit highly limited, support for multilateral approaches to various Asian security issues, primarily intended to allay fears concerning China's future military and diplomatic intentions toward Asia while minimizing constraints on Chinese behavior

- Support for the full resumption of official political and military dialogues and exchanges with the United States and its allies, combined with limited concessions on major U.S. concerns such as human rights, arms sales, and trade

- Maintenance of positive relations with the Central Asian republics and major centers of Islamic fundamentalism such as Iran, through enhanced trade and investment links, expanding diplomatic ties, and Chinese assistance in critical development areas, including nuclear power.

---

[8]Hence, this tenet partly counterbalances the previous tenet's stress on maintaining good relations with the United States. It should also be noted that many Chinese and foreign observers recognize that the post–Cold War triangle is not a true strategic configuration, given the major power asymmetries of the participants.

3. *Continued significant levels of funding for conventional military modernization, aimed at the creation of a modern force structure and operational doctrine.*[9]

This tenet derives from the military requirements of China's post–Cold War security environment, which posit the development of a relatively small, highly trained and motivated, mobile, versatile, and well-coordinated air, land, and sea force in support of a new defense doctrine centered on the concepts of local war, active peripheral defense, and rapid power projection.[10] Such a force requires technologically advanced weapons with medium- and long-range force projection, rapid reaction, and offshore maneuverability capabilities and a modern, combined services tactical operations doctrine employing sophisticated C3I systems.[11] This diverse set of military capabilities requires, in turn, a host of support features, including a more robust research and development capability, a more technologically advanced and quality-driven defense industry, and a highly professionalized, merit-based system of officer recruitment, promotion, and training.[12]

China's new force structure and defense doctrine emerged primarily in response to the collapse of the Soviet threat in the mid eighties, the largely negative experience of the costly border war with Vietnam in 1979, and the overwhelming and rapid victory of U.S. forces over a

---

[9]As a secondary priority, this feature also likely involves the development of tactical nuclear weapons and the improvement of the survivability, penetration, and retaliation capacity of China's strategic nuclear forces.

[10]Such notions are based, in turn, upon several recently accepted military principles and combat methods, including a revised concept of "strategic frontier," and the notions of "strategic deterrence," and "gaining the initiative by striking first." For definitions of these concepts, see Swaine (forthcoming). Also see Nan Li, "War Doctrine, Strategic Principles and Operational Concepts of the People's Liberation Army: New Developments (1985–1993)," unpublished paper, pp. 7–14, and Paul H. B. Godwin, "Changing Concepts of Doctrine, Strategy, and Operations in the People's Liberation Army 1978–87," *The China Quarterly*, No. 112, December 1987, pp. 573–590.

[11]Specifically, the Chinese now place a high priority on the development of airborne drop and amphibious landing capabilities, air and naval electronic warfare systems, improved missile and aircraft guidance systems, precision-guided munitions, the construction of communications and early warning satellites, and the acquisition of in-flight refueling technologies.

[12]For a detailed summary of China's major weapons acquisitions, both recent and planned, see Swaine et al. (forthcoming).

large Soviet and Chinese-armed Iraqi force during the Gulf War of 1991. In addition, many of the above changes derive from the new security requirements presented by China's emergence during the past decade as a major trading nation, with expanding oceanic links and growing external dependencies, as well as the leadership's need, following the Tiananmen incident, to develop rapid deployment forces for use in quelling domestic social unrest.[13]

Together, such developments confirmed to Chinese military planners that the time-honored concept of People's War, keyed to the use of massive ground forces in a protracted conflict on the Asian mainland, and a force structure primarily dependent upon technologies of the fifties and sixties are completely inadequate for dealing with the external and internal security challenges of the twenty-first century. As a result, China has undergone a fundamental transformation in strategic outlook, from a continental power primarily concerned with threats to its internal borders, to a combined continental/maritime power with a much wider range of domestic and external security needs.

Specifically, China's new force structure and doctrine is intended to satisfy at least five major strategic requirements:

- To increase China's overall global and regional stature, particularly through the display of high-technology weaponry and efforts to "show the flag" beyond China's borders

- To deal with the uncertain future military postures of the United States, Japan, the ASEAN states, and perhaps India

- To maintain a credible threat of force toward an increasingly separatist-minded and economically potent Taiwan

- To improve Chinese military and diplomatic leverage over and access to nearby strategic territories claimed by Beijing, such as in the South China Sea, and to defend access to vital oceanic routes in the event of conflict

- To strengthen China's ability to deal with domestic social unrest and ethnically based border instabilities.

---

[13]For further details, see Swaine (forthcoming).

This tenet obviously serves many purposes central to the interests of China's political and military leadership, especially the professional military and specific service arms such as the Chinese Navy and Air Force. Although its central components include elements of the hardline, conservative variant of the mainstream view of the regional environment, it also relies in large part on maintaining good relations with major foreign sources of advanced military technology and expertise such as the United States and Russia.

4. *Efforts to sell both sophisticated and low-technology arms and arms-related equipment, including "big ticket" items such as ballistic missiles and nuclear technology.*

This tenet is closely related to the previous one. It is linked to Beijing's efforts to augment both military and central government revenues, increase its diplomatic and strategic leverage against the United States and other potential antagonists, and assist important allies such as Pakistan. However, strong incentives exist to avoid extreme actions in this area that would jeopardize other essential tenets of China's strategy, such as the creation of a stable regional and global environment and the maintenance of good relations with the West. The Ministry of Foreign Affairs (MoFA) probably serves as the major proponent, in high party and military circles, of the need for such restraint,[14] while progressives may go so far as to support privately the virtual elimination of major arms and nuclear technology sales. However, at present, the Chinese military and the senior party leadership probably play a dominant, if not exclusive, role in determining and implementing this tenet of China's foreign policy. Moreover, military proponents of the hardline, or "neo-conservative," variant of the mainstream approach almost certainly support it and probably resist any interference from the MoFA. Overall, such significant differences suggest a basis for future leadership conflict over this tenet.

---

[14]For example, many MoFA officials oppose the sale of intermediate ballistic missiles and nuclear technology that clearly violates IAEA guidelines (in contrast to tactical ballistic missiles, missile components, and IAEA-sanctioned technologies). For a recent overview of China's foreign missile and nuclear technology policy and sales, see Jonathan D. Pollack, "China and Asia's Nuclear Future," in Francine Frankel (ed.), *Bridging the Nonproliferation Divide: The United States and India*, the University Press of America, Lanham, Maryland, 1995, pp. 98–119.

5. *Increased cultural, economic, and political interactions with Taiwan, combined with continued efforts to maintain the credibility of the possible use of force to reunify the country and to avoid the emergence of a "two Chinas" situation.*

 This tenet is closely linked to all three of China's basic foreign policy priorities and is highly valued by both the military and civilian leadership. It derives from a strong desire to eventually "absorb" Taiwan peacefully through a process of economic, and ultimately political, convergence made possible by a rapidly developing mainland and the continued deterrence of the de facto emergence of an independent Taiwan. The key elements of this approach include:

- The creation of a strong Taiwanese stake in good relations and continued economic ties with the mainland

- The maintenance of pressure on other (especially Asian) states to avoid de facto recognition of an independent Taiwan

- The prevention of Taiwanese participation in any international activities that connote political sovereignty, such as multilateral security discussions and arrangements[15]

- The avoidance of undue military provocation against Taiwan, combined with the preservation of the credibility of a possible Chinese use of force to reunify the country.

As with the previous tenet, however, this tenet is also closely associated with the interests of the Chinese military (which could exert significant influence over its development in the future), as well as civilian hardliners. Among these groups, a growing number of individuals are pressing for a much tougher stance toward Taiwan. On the other hand, progressives among foreign policy strategists and officials might privately support a more conciliatory approach, perhaps including support for Taiwan's admission to the United Nations (following the East/West Germany and North/South Korea formulas), acceptance of the concept of "one country, two governments" espoused by Taipei, and even perhaps an eventual abandonment or

---

[15]This element partly explains China's highly suspicious stance toward any U.S. leadership role in such fora. Beijing believes such a role could lead to efforts by Washington to include Taiwan in regional security dialogues.

modification of the Chinese threat of force. Unfortunately, however, this viewpoint appears to be losing whatever influence it may have had among the Chinese leadership.

6. *Pursuit of a cautious but firm approach to the Spratly Islands issue.*

This tenet is potentially associated with all three of China's basic foreign policy priorities but currently is most closely identified with the second and third priorities.

The central elements of this tenet include:

- A stress on the settlement of all territorial disputes by peaceful means and on a bilateral basis

- Strong opposition to the formation of any formal international organization for handling such disputes

- Insistence on Chinese sovereignty over the entire Spratly Islands chain

- A willingness to set aside the sovereignty issue to explore various types of international cooperation mechanisms for joint exploration and development of the area's resources.

The main lines of this relatively cautious approach reflect the influence of the Ministry of Foreign Affairs, which desires to prevent tensions over the Spratlys from threatening the priority on continued economic development through outward-oriented reform. Of greatest urgency, from the ministry's perspective, is to avoid the emergence of a "united front" within ASEAN in opposition to China's claims to the islands. Such a confrontation could undermine China's growing economic and diplomatic ties to Southeast Asia. Specifically, foreign ministry strategists and officials reportedly insist that a more assertive Chinese stance toward the Spratlys would weaken China's ability to use close ties with ASEAN to counter possible future tensions with both the United States and Japan.[16] However, this issue also directly involves the interests of the Chinese military. The Chinese Navy in particular has taken a direct role in

---

[16]Vietnam's impending entrance into ASEAN will likely complicate this strategy, however, since Beijing has shown a willingness to employ military force in the past to rebuff Hanoi's claims to the area.

pushing a more assertive Chinese stance toward the Spratlys, thus producing confrontations with the MoFA in the past.[17] Ideological conservatives within both the civilian and military leadership also apparently support the navy's approach. Progressives almost certainly oppose it, however, along with many civilian strategists and apparently a significant number of military officers in the ground forces. Such bureaucratic and ideological differences thus place the existing policy on a potentially precarious basis, arguably to a much greater degree than in the case of policy toward Taiwan.

7. *Efforts to avoid either a nuclearized Korea or a rapid reunification of the peninsula through a sudden collapse of the North, combined with efforts to strengthen economic, political, and diplomatic ties with South Korea, both for developmental reasons, and in anticipation of its likely absorption of the North.*

This tenet is strongly connected to the first basic priority in China's security strategy, given the obvious dangers that a nuclear Korea or conflict on the Korean peninsula would pose for China's outward-oriented economic reform effort, as well as the benefits that the Chinese economy would receive from a prosperous, unified, and friendly Korea. China's strategic interests are also central to this tenet, however. For example, the establishment of close relations with a unified Korea would serve to augment Beijing's diplomatic and political leverage over Japan, given the historical frictions existing between Tokyo and Seoul. Alternatively, Beijing also fears that a crisis on the Korean peninsula could stimulate Japanese remilitarization or cause Japan to develop a theater missile defense shield, thereby eroding the possible deterrent effect against Tokyo of

---

[17]For example, in early 1992, the MoFA reportedly favored a vague Chinese policy statement from the National People's Congress that would have shelved the question of sovereignty over the islands for an indefinite period. This position was rejected in favor of a less conciliatory stance, however, in part because of pressures from the navy. The result was the rather provocative NPC "law" of February 1992, which laid claim to the entire area and suggested a Chinese willingness to use force to defend it. The role of General Liu Huaqing, currently a member of the Politburo Standing Committee and a close associate of Deng Xiaoping, could prove decisive in the future, since he has been centrally involved as a proponent of both a blue-water navy and Chinese advances into the South China Sea. See John W. Garver, "China's Push Through the South China Sea: The Interaction of Bureaucratic and National Interests," *China Quarterly*, No. 132, December 1992.

China's small nuclear force. This tenet is also affected by concerns over the implications of a U.S.-induced North Korean collapse for the stability and legitimacy of the Chinese socialist regime, and strong suspicions that U.S. efforts to press North Korea to accept major restrictions on its nuclear program will eventually be directed against China. At the same time, Beijing also wishes to prevent developments on the Korean peninsula from exacerbating Sino-U.S. tensions. Finally, from a longer-term perspective, this tenet is also influenced by concerns over future territorial disputes with a reunified Korea.

These many, often conflicting aims make this tenet of China's regional security strategy perhaps the most complex for Beijing to implement. It requires walking a fine line between (a) support for international efforts to ensure a nonnuclear peninsula and the gradual, peaceful transition to a unified Korea with close ties to Beijing, and (b) continued efforts to avoid isolating or provoking the North Korean regime to drastic action. As a result, serious differences over Korea policy could emerge within China's successor leadership over the medium to long term, aggravating existing internal frictions in other policy areas.

8. *Increasing economic and diplomatic interactions with Inner Asia, to forestall a rapid and destabilizing expansion in Islamic fundamentalism originating from neighboring Muslim states.*

This tenet is most directly associated with both the first and second basic priorities in China's overall security strategy. That is, stability on China's western borders is essential to national unity and the continued maintenance of a placid external environment conducive to economic reform. China's rapid economic development provides a strong incentive for the largely impoverished Islamic republics of the former USSR to expand trade and investment ties with Beijing rather than to encourage the separatist activities of the Muslim minorities in China's Xinjiang province.[18]   Hence, China's policy stresses efforts to strengthen the stake of its Inner Asian neighbors in

---

[18]The pull of the Chinese economic magnet is all the stronger because of the generally poor economic conditions prevailing in such major non-Russian alternative sources of influence over the republics as Turkey and Iran.

economic reform and close economic and political relations with Beijing, not to project political influence across the border.[19] This pragmatic policy also applies to Beijing's relations with more distant centers of Islamic fundamentalism such as Iran. This tenet is strongly supported by both the Ministry of Foreign Affairs and the Chinese military. However, as with policy toward the Spratly Islands, the activities of the latter could lead to increased tensions within neighboring Inner Asian states in the future, especially if China's relative economic advantage in the region declines and problems emerge in the leadership succession process.

The above three fundamental foreign policy priorities and resulting eight tenets of security strategy suggest a basis for future Chinese caution and pragmatism toward both the Asia-Pacific region and the West. In other words, the strongly status- and power-oriented (and potentially destabilizing) nationalistic impulses motivating certain core elements of China's strategic approach will probably be restrained by the imperative of maintaining continued high levels of economic growth through outward-oriented, market-led reform, at least over the medium term (i.e., 5–10 years). This implies a continued balanced Chinese approach toward the United States in particular, combining elements of both cooperation and competition, along with a generally risk-averse stance toward potential troublespots in the Asia-Pacific region. Such an approach provides few incentives for significant levels of adverse Chinese behavior toward the region beyond those that currently exist, e.g., problems or tensions over arms and technology sales, market access, and territorial issues.

However, China's continued implementation of the above largely cautious, pragmatic, and balanced security strategy does not preclude the possibility of more serious problems emerging *over the long term*. The central tenets of China's regional security stance are not those of a status quo power. They assume the eventual expansion of Chinese influence or direct control over nearby territories claimed by other Asian countries, as well as a greatly increased ability to shape events across much of the Asia-Pacific region, through the

---

[19]As a result of these policies, Xinjiang is now growing as quickly as southern provinces such as Guangdong. See Overholt (1993), p. 354. Also see Bonnie S. Glaser, "China's Security Perceptions: Interests and Ambitions," *Asian Survey*, Vol. 33, No. 3, March 1993, pp. 252–271.

combined use of more potent economic, military, and diplomatic instruments of national power. Beijing's growing capabilities[20] could
thus interact with its general desire to exert greater influence over
events in the region to produce an increasingly intense climate of
uncertainty and anxiety concerning China's ultimate motives, even
in the absence of aggressive or highly nationalistic Chinese behavior.
This climate could eventually precipitate an escalating, negative
pattern of interaction between China and many regional powers
(including the United States), possibly resulting in a highly dangerous arms race or a variety of destabilizing diplomatic (or even military) confrontations.

This is the most likely form of adversity that could emerge from the
continuation of the above central tenets of China's security stance
over the long term. Yet it would also likely prove to be the most
manageable or avoidable form of adversity, since it involves the
gradual accretion of power by Beijing and the *gradual* emergence or
intensification of mutual misunderstandings. Under such circumstances, the most serious difficulties would most likely result from
major miscommunications between China and critical foreign countries such as the United States as well as from specific foreign actions
deemed "provocative" by the Chinese. This suggests a need for the
United States and major regional powers to establish stronger and
more extensive lines of communication with China's military and
civilian leaderships and to make clear the likely costs and benefits
that would result from specific forms of assertive or cooperative
Chinese behavior.[21]

However, even assuming such positive actions were undertaken by
outside powers, highly adverse Chinese behavior might still result
from domestic factors. For example, in an effort to consolidate
power and avert any chance of social instability following the death
of Deng Xiaoping, China's successor leadership might be forced to
placate the military and respond to increasing conservative nationalist sentiments in the polity and society by taking a less cooperative

---

[20]This outcome of course assumes that Beijing will solve its pressing economic reform
problems and avoid a prolonged or severe succession struggle after the passing of
Deng Xiaoping. The possible consequences of the failure of either or both of these
assumptions are discussed below.

[21]More on these points in Chapter Six.

stance toward a range of such issues as the acquisition of defense technologies, military spending, and arms transfers. Moreover, enhanced military influence over central government policies might prompt the Chinese Navy to intensify its past efforts to use China's external maritime policies to justify stronger central support and bigger budgets for the development of a modern, technically proficient, combat-ready blue water capability. This could lead to a more assertive policy toward both the Spratlys and perhaps Taiwan.[22] Such increased military influence over foreign policy could also accelerate China's efforts to obtain military assistance and equipment from Russia, for example, thus creating greater concerns in the West.[23]

However, one should not overemphasize the likelihood of such scenarios. The civilian successor leadership will probably manage to resist excessive military influence over foreign policy, and particularly the influence of hardline conservatives, as long as the major political, social, and economic incentives underlying China's existing foreign policy priorities remain in place. Barring a complete breakdown of cooperation among the successor leadership, a major economic crisis, or the emergence of a major external threat, leading civilian bureaucratic-technocrats will likely resist pressures for more direct military intervention in foreign policy by appealing to moderate, professional military views supportive of the military's detachment from politics, the need to maintain strong economic ties with capitalist states, and anticipated future increases in diplomatic and economic leverage against the West as China grows stronger and avoids major external crises. In this effort, Jiang Zemin and his associates or other senior members of the successor leadership who might supplant Jiang would be expected to rely upon such key military allies as General Zhang Zhen (assuming he is still active) and Defense Minister Chi Haotian. Finally, such an effort would be greatly facili-

---

[22]However, barring a major provocation from Taiwan, it is more likely that the Spratlys would be used as an issue in domestic politics, rather than the Taiwan problem. The Spratlys involve less-capable opponents, a lower risk of U.S. military intervention, and a lesser threat to China's economic ties with Japan and Korea.

[23]According to several analysts, the Chinese military has been much more interested in signing a sales contract and increasing its external influence and domestic power base than in averting foreign policy crises in areas such as the Spratlys and foreign arms sales. See, for example, Lewis et al. (1991), pp. 87–109.

tated if better lines of communication existed between Chinese and foreign leaders.

IMPLICATIONS OF DISCONTINUITY

Far more potentially dangerous consequences for the United States and Asia could result from certain *discontinuities* in China's existing security or foreign policy stance. Such discontinuities, largely involving a major reduction in China's willingness to maintain cooperative relations with the West, could lead to actions that threaten regional stability and economic growth in sudden or extremely severe ways. At least two such adverse Chinese policy stances could emerge over the next 10–15 years, each resulting from different combinations of outcomes associated with the above domestic political, social, and economic trends and features. The first presents a largely offensive startegic stance, while the second is largely defensive in nature, yet still highly destabilizing.

Alternative One: A Highly Assertive China, Committed to Regional Dominance

The major tenets of this external policy stance include:

• The use of growing power-projection abilities and increased regional economic clout to intimidate or greatly influence the actions of smaller states, including Korea and the ASEAN countries

• Increased challenges to U.S. interests (e.g., regarding regional or bilateral trade, Taiwan, counterproliferation, human rights, and policy toward Japan and Russia)

• More concerted attempts to reduce external economic dependencies by diversifying foreign economic relations, exerting greater controls over foreign economic activities in China, and developing a strong domestic market.

Such potentially provocative or tension-producing behavior would largely result from a reordering of the three basic principles guiding China's overall foreign policy and security stance. Specifically, the priority emphasis on rapid civilian economic growth would give way to the state-centered nationalist goals of the defense of national sovereignty and territory and the attainment of big-power status. This would likely lead to a foreign policy largely centered on the views of hardliners, including expectations of more local conflicts, escalating arms competition in the region, increased challenges to claimed territories, heightened fears over Japan's reemergence as a military power, instabilities in Inner Asia, and especially increased U.S. (and perhaps other Western) efforts to restrain China's development.

A combination of at least three domestic factors would increase the chances of such a fundamentally adverse shift in Chinese foreign policy:

- Stable, high growth rates with manageable inflation

- A fiscally strong central government

- A high level of conservative (especially military) involvement in politics.

The maintenance of high, stable growth rates with tolerable levels of inflation would likely require a deepening of China's reform effort, involving the successful implementation of an effective national taxation system, monetary stabilization, currency convertibility, property rights, and the further liberalization of labor markets, as well as China's further integration into world markets. Many of these actions would depend, in turn, on the resolution or avoidance of fundamental structural and other problems in the Chinese economy. Taken together, these actions would likely provide the basis for a very high level of self-confidence in foreign affairs and an increased ability to support high levels of military modernization. The latter would be especially likely if state revenues for the military were augmented by increased levels of income derived from business ventures, through an expansion of the trend toward military involvement in the economy.

However, such economic developments alone would not necessarily lead to *rapid* increases in Chinese military capabilities and a much more *assertive* regional posture, given the strong disincentives that would likely persist against such potentially dangerous behavior, at least over the next 10–15 years. The emergence of Alternative One would also require a major increase in the direct influence of conservative hardline leadership groups over Chinese foreign policy, especially those associated with the military. *Such conservative military influence would be far more direct and intense than the form of influence posited under the scenario of policy continuity discussed above.*

In a context of significant economic success, conservative military influence over internal and external policies would become possible largely as a result of a prolonged and severe power struggle among the senior civilian leadership. The critical indicators of such conservative military intervention would likely include:

- An escalating succession struggle, resulting in policy paralysis or confusion, despite the above economic successes

- Thinly veiled public appeals by conservative civilian successors to their putative counterparts within the military, advocating a more assertive, nationalistic domestic and foreign policy line[24]

- A marked reduction in public references to more moderate, cooperative policies basic to the mainstream foreign policy approach, and a gradual but clear increase in reference to assertive nationalist themes

- Efforts by conservative factions within the military to unite a conflictual successor leadership and reduce the chances of social pressure on the regime by seizing control of the government; this, in turn, would be indicated by

- Major increases in the number of leading military figures holding top posts within central party and state organs, especially those known to support conservative foreign policy views.

In bullet two, some putative successors might attempt to increase their standing among military conservatives and all those committed to order as a first priority, while others might seek to garner the support of more moderate or progressive military (and civilian) leaders. In such a contest, conservatives in particular would be strongly tempted to use foreign policy issues to garner greater support, given the nationalistic and often xenophobic attitudes of the populace and

---

[24]Here the political motives and calculations of contending civilian and military leaders—especially the remaining "retired" military elders and the failed aspirants to power such as Yang Shangkun—would likely prove decisive.

of groups within the military.[25] In bullet four, unified, conservative military intervention would become more likely if several influential retired military elders remained on the scene. These individuals could pressure their "subordinates" within the formal military hierarchy to directly intervene in politics and would probably also serve to maintain unity within the military throughout the process.

One should not assume that such internal developments would inevitably lead to Alternative One, however. Under conditions of sustained economic growth and fiscal solvency, it is doubtful that a succession struggle alone would negate, for a prolonged period of time, the many factors currently supporting the moderate and balanced views of mainstream military and civilian leaders. Indeed, the above scenario suggests a largely episodic or sporadic pattern of conservative influence over foreign policy, dependent upon the continued presence of elder leaders and the general severity and longevity of the leadership conflict. Moderates within the military, with the assistance of their civilian counterparts, might ultimately hold sway and check the influence of conservatives, given the obvious threats to continued economic stability and social order posed by a more assertive, hardline foreign policy.

Given such considerations, it appears that a shift to Alternative One would probably also require *external* stimuli, in the form of supposedly "provocative" behavior by key foreign countries such as the United States, Japan, or Russia. During a severe leadership struggle, such behavior would likely increase exponentially the persuasiveness of conservative views, weaken the arguments of mainstream moderates, and eventually produce a prolonged and long-lasting pattern of assertive Chinese external behavior.

Variant: An even more destabilizing version of Alternative One could emerge over the long term, involving a highly assertive pattern of Chinese behavior in three specific foreign policy areas critical to military interests: foreign trade, arms sales, and territorial claims. This would result largely from increased military involvement in foreign policy, perhaps associated with a prolonged succession struggle as

---

[25]In addition, the handling of the Tiananmen demonstrations and their aftermath could also become a key issue of debate in such a confrontation.

above, but under conditions of high growth *combined with severe fiscal constraints.*

The leadership's continued failure to ensure adequate tax revenues for the central government, despite a growing economy, would likely lower the growth of public spending well below the GNP growth rate over the long term. This could ultimately constrain the center's ability to maintain reasonably high rates of military funding. Such a crisis could lead, especially in a post-Deng succession struggle, to concerted military efforts to significantly increase revenues earmarked for force modernization. Specifically, under severe fiscal pressures, the military could argue for:

- Stronger central government controls over foreign trade and investment, intended to accumulate greater amounts of foreign exchange

- Increased reliance on the foreign sale of expensive arms (e.g., short- and medium-range ballistic missiles) and nuclear technology

- More determined efforts to assert Chinese control over the actual and potential oil, gas, and fish reserves of the Spratly Islands.[26]

Support for the above types of increased, direct military intervention in foreign policy would be particularly strong among those military leaders most concerned with defending professionalism against the corrosive effects of military capitalism. Such officers might urge the above policies to reduce the military's reliance on both legitimate and illegitimate business practices as a means of compensating for declining state revenues. Moreover, such military professionals could receive support from the more ideological views of foreign policy conservatives, as well as some conservative bureaucratic technocrats among the successor leadership.[27]

---

[26]This goal could generate considerable increases in state revenues while it reduces China's dependence on foreign economic ties.

[27]This view could also find strong support among some strongly reformist civilian leaders if the levels of economic corruption in the military reached alarmingly high levels over the long term.

Alternatively, the emergence of an acute fiscal crisis impinging on military modernization could lead to an explosion in profit-making activities by the military. This, in turn, could greatly aggravate corruption and lawlessness within China and also produce a variety of severe economic tensions with the United States and other important trade and investment partners. These problems might also precipitate an open conflict between military professionals and military capitalists, with neither side in the ascendance. Such a conflict could lead to the formation of broad, opposing civil-military coalitions between military capitalists, civilian progressives, and provincial/municipal political and business elites on the one side, and military professionals and conservatives, civilian conservatives, and inland provincial/municipal leaders on the other. These conflict scenarios would likely result in a period of prolonged instability within both civilian and military leaderships, with consequences for China's regional posture similar to those of Alternative Two, below.[28]

The critical domestic indicators of this adverse scenario would likely include:

- The failure to implement a genuinely effective program of national tax reform designed to assure a stable and increasing level of revenues for the central government, commensurate with overall national growth levels

- Prolonged, declining levels of official government spending on military modernization and other military-related activities, manifested either as a constant defense budget, or a defense budget growing slower than military costs[29]

- Greatly increased media presentations of military views on foreign trade, arms sales, and territorial claims issues, or on its various legitimate and illegitimate business activities

---

[28]Moreover, if the nature and extent of the military's business activities produce strong links between local military establishments and specific regional elites, such as those in the coastal areas, such instability could greatly heighten internal regional tensions. Such a scenario might eventually produce similar external consequences to the "worst case" variant of Alternative Two.

[29]Increased productivity elsewhere in the economy will require pay to grow faster than inflation for officers and ordinary soldiers. Thus, a budget that only keeps up with inflation will likely reduce military force structure.

- Media signals of a growing debate between military capitalists and military professionals, with indications of support from specific types of central and local civilian leaders.

The behavior of foreign countries could also greatly influence the likelihood of this variant's occurrence. For example, a prior escalation of tensions in the South China Sea involving "provocative" actions by other claimants such as Vietnam or the Philippines, the adoption of a more punitive, high-pressure approach by the United States regarding Chinese arms and nuclear technology sales, and generally increasing economic tensions with Japan, the United States, or other major Chinese economic partners could all serve to reduce both military and civilian leadership resistance to the three types of assertive Chinese foreign policy behavior characteristic of Alternative One.

Alternative Two: A Weak, Insecure, and Defensive China, Concerned with Preventing Foreign Intervention or Social Chaos

The major tenets of this alternative approach include:

- The clear identification of Japan or the United States as a major threat to Chinese security

- Greatly increased concerns over challenges to Chinese territory, perhaps leading to major deployments of military forces in the Spratlys

- A more suspicious/hostile stance toward Western-sponsored positions in the United Nations and other international fora

- Increasing pressures on Taiwan and Hong Kong

- Greater efforts to reassert central control over foreign economic activities, involving more repressive government policies.

Such a dramatic, directly threatening shift in Chinese foreign policy behavior would most likely result from a period of prolonged economic decline or stagnation, combined with severe leadership conflict and/or paralysis, yet an avoidance of complete social collapse or national fragmentation. Some Sinologists believe such a development is the most probable *worst case* outcome over the long term.[30] It would most likely derive from complete failures in several key areas of domestic reform, along with an uncontrollable power struggle. Such problems could lead to escalating factionalism, provincial indiscipline, popular political antipathy, government financial problems, and bureaucratic footdragging, thus resulting in a serious economic downturn and a political leadership crisis.

Under such a situation, factions supporting either more radical reform or conservative retrenchment might compete for the support of various provinces. However, in such a chaotic environment, provinces would be highly inclined to follow their own policies, spending and credit could escalate out of control, and inflation would likely accelerate. Each province and major city would probably then resort to protectionist measures, leading to further economic decline and political conflict.[31] Such negative developments would be further intensified if China's successor bureaucratic technocratic leadership continued to exclude from the central government leading representatives of political and business circles from the more dynamic coastal areas.

In this precarious environment, some civilian leaders might calculate that the adoption of a more assertive ultra-nationalist foreign policy stance (including the creation or claim of a severe foreign threat to China from Japan or the United States) would elicit greater military support, unify the political system and the populace behind the cause of patriotic nationalism, and divert public attention from the declining domestic economy. This policy could eventually lead to even greater leadership disarray, however, and perhaps direct, destabilizing military intervention in politics. China's resulting external policy stance might thus share some of the attributes of Alternative One but would almost certainly be far more unstable and potentially aggressive, involving sudden or sharp confrontations with the West. Unlike Alternative One, such a stance would display highly

---

[30]For example, see Overholt (1993), p. 112–113, and David M. Lampton, "China's Biggest Problem: Gridlock, Not Revolution," in *China's Economic Dilemmas in the 1990's: The Problems of Reforms, Modernization, and Interdependence*, study papers submitted to the Joint Economic Committee, Congress of the United States, U.S. Government Printing Office, Washington, D.C., 1991, pp. 65–69.

[31]Overholt (1993), pp. 113–114.

defensive and insecure behavior, including, perhaps, attempts at pre-emptive military action. This behavior derives from the widespread belief, held by many Chinese leaders, that a weakened Chinese state invites foreign aggression.

The most critical domestic indicators of this adverse scenario would likely involve the following:

- The failure of the successor leadership to establish a consensus on dealing with a range of obstacles to the final stages of economic reform, such as the future disposition of huge state enterprises, the establishment of a more effective national banking system, and an effective program of national tax reform

- The inability to generate future growth through expansion of the domestic economy and utilization of China's very high domestic savings, rather than a continued reliance on exports

- A lack of confidence in the economy by China's emerging entrepreneurs, manifested by slackening investment in the private sector; the first visible sign of this lack of faith would probably be an upsurge in the flight of capital

- A domestic power struggle as in Alternative One, leading to the emergence of the (neo-)conservative, hardline viewpoint on China's security environment as the new "mainstream" view.

Foreign events could also play a decisive role in producing this external policy stance. For example, a severe downturn of the global economy would greatly increase the likelihood of major economic decline or stagnation in China. More directly, increasing foreign protectionism or severe trade tensions with key Chinese economic partners such as the United States and Japan could also produce severe economic problems, especially if China were unable to diversify its foreign markets or to strengthen and unify its domestic market for Chinese products. Moreover, several types of supposedly "provocative" behavior by foreign countries would almost certainly increase greatly the Chinese sense of threat and vulnerability, thus producing a defensive backlash. In addition to those foreign actions mentioned under Alternative One, such behavior might include harsh U.S. economic sanctions or a confrontation with the United States over Taiwan or Hong Kong. The latter would be particularly likely to produce Alternative Two, given the close association of these territorial issues with Western aggression against China. Another less obvious form of provocative foreign behavior would consist of efforts by foreign countries to manipulate differences among China's contending central and subnational leaderships to increase diplomatic or economic leverage against Beijing. Such actions have been encouraged by some foreign observers of the Chinese scene, but would be highly dangerous, even under conditions of stable Chinese economic growth.

Variant: A "worst case" variant of the above alternative could also occur. This would involve external behavior similar in some respects to a weak, insecure, defensive China, but combined with:

- The likely emergence, among many provinces or regions, of highly independent external economic policies

- A mass exodus of refugees to neighboring states and regions

- Major ethnic unrest along China's western borders.

This variant of the above alternative would derive from an extremely chaotic domestic situation, resulting from a period of *prolonged and very severe* economic and social decline, exacerbated by unresolved (and possibly violent) conflicts among both civilian and military successor leaderships at the central level. Moreover, such a dangerous scenario could draw subnational conservative and more pro-reform officials into the conflict and might even lead, under certain circumstances, to the sporadic use of regional forces in support of contending factions.[32] Such severe instability would be especially likely if no party or military elders remained on the political stage to maintain discipline and unity among younger civilian and military leaders.

The most critical domestic indicators of this adverse scenario would likely include those presented initially in Alternative Two, exacerbated by:

---

[32]For further details on this scenario, see Michael D. Swaine, "Chinese Regional Forces as Political Actors," in Richard H. Yang, Jason C. Hu, Peter Kien-hong Yu, and Andrew N.D. Yang (eds.), *Chinese Regionalism: The Security Dimension*, Westview Press, Boulder, Colorado, April 1994.

- Negative economic growth rates over several years, if not nationally at least in several regions of the nation

- Stockpiling and widespread shortages of goods moved in interprovincial trade, particularly those regulated by the center

- A collapse of the tax collection system; reactions to such a problem could include greatly accelerated inflation or sporadic and reduced pay for central and local government employees

- An exchange rate in free-fall and the collapse of normal trade relations; China's trading partners would become loath to extend credit and would insist on foreign currency; exporters would be scrambling to unload merchandise to acquire foreign exchange, preferably in an overseas account

- Accelerated efforts by individual provinces or regions to adopt independent or protectionist fiscal, trade, and investment polities, perhaps leading to

- Open provincial or municipal defiance of central directives and regulations

- The weakening of government programs to limit the rate of urbanization or urban population growth

- Increasing indications of social unrest in China's cities, including public demonstrations against the government.

Moreover, as in Alternative Two, many external economic and political events could greatly exacerbate such a situation.

Whether this situation would eventually result in a complete collapse of the Chinese state and a totally chaotic, fragmented pattern of relations with the outside is a subject of intense debate among specialists inside and outside China. This issue cannot be resolved here. However, the following factors would likely inhibit the complete breakup of China, even under conditions of the most extreme domestic political and social chaos:[33]

---

[33]Many of the following points are taken from Overholt (1993), p. 101, and Sutter et al. (1993), pp. 10–11.

- A highly homogeneous ethnic population[34]

- A strong and deeply rooted sense of history

- A firm sense of national identity

- Central controls over critical regional economic and administrative resources

- Central controls over key provincial personnel

- An increasingly professional, centralized system of military leadership and organization.

Alternative Three: A "Normal" China, Pursuing Much Greater Cooperation with the West

Specific key tenets of this approach would likely include:

- Support for most Western security goals, and the termination of efforts to maximize strategic independence and leverage through the manipulation of relations between the United States and its key allies

- A shared leadership role in regional multilateral economic and security fora

- Support for a loose confederation with Taiwan, maximum freedom for Hong Kong, and joint development of the Spratlys.

Such a positive transformation in China's security stance toward the Asia-Pacific region and the West is not likely, particularly over the near and medium term. Its emergence would probably require a combination of many internal factors, each an indicator of this scenario:

---

[34]In contrast to the situation in the former Soviet Union, well over 90 percent of China's population are from a single ethnic group: the Han Chinese. Although the vast majority of China's minority ethnic groups are concentrated primarily in sensitive border areas, thus posing potential problems for the government, they are usually heavily interspersed with Han Chinese and under the tight control of local military forces.

- The resolution of China's basic reform problems, producing sustained rates of moderate economic growth
- The absence of a destabilizing succession struggle
- The emergence of a reasonably cohesive post-succession collective leadership dominated by radical civilian reformers, military businessmen, military and security policy progressives, and private business elites.

Many of these events are highly problematic yet could occur over the long term under a "best case" scenario. They would greatly increase the likelihood that conservative military elements will stay out of politics and that strong incentives will remain on maintaining close ties with the outside and continued cooperation with developed countries. Under such positive conditions, an array of policy progressives and business-oriented military and civilian leaders might be able to exert greater influence over foreign affairs. Specifically, the position of radical civilian reformers in Beijing (especially those seeking to minimize conservative military and civilian influence over the post-Deng leadership) would be strengthened and closer links forged with provincial and local leaders in the dynamic coastal areas. Moreover, military figures who gain the most from private business activities could press for a greater reliance on obtaining needed revenues for force modernization through enhanced defense conversion and closer ties with the coastal economies. Such individuals might link up with military progressives and nonmainstream foreign policy strategists and officials to argue for less direct interference by Beijing in regional affairs, the avoidance of big-ticket arms sales, and less military involvement in those types of external behavior that threaten continued outward-oriented economic growth.

In addition to these internal factors, movement toward such an unprecedented Chinese security stance would also likely require significant external precipitants, including even greater reliance on extensive trade, investment, and technology ties with Asia and the West, the absence of strongly provocative economic, military, or diplomatic actions by the United States, the emergence of constructive, positive-sum interactions with many Asian countries (on both a bilateral and multilateral basis), and the avoidance of significant confrontations over territorial issues such as the Spratly Islands, Taiwan, Tibet, and the the Sino-Indian and Sino-Russian borders. In addition, in this context, the emergence of a competitive Sino-Japanese economic relationship would likely provide additional incentives for China to establish close economic and political ties with the United States and other Asian countries.[35]

---

[35]Such a relatively positive outcome for the United States assumes that the U.S.-Japan security relationship would remain intact, thereby preventing increasing Sino-Japanese economic rivalry from leading to a destabilizing military rivalry.

Chapter Six

IMPLICATIONS FOR THE UNITED STATES

This study was not designed to formulate detailed recommendations for future U.S. policy toward China and the Asia-Pacific region. However, several broad implications for U.S. policy follow from the above analysis.

First, domestic change in China will almost certainly not result in a significantly more democratic and pro-Western Chinese regime over the next 10–15 years; neither, however, will it likely lead to the emergence of independent regional power centers or the complete breakdown of political rule in China. During this period, most Chinese will remain primarily concerned over increasing economic corruption, crime and social unrest, lingering poverty, and unfair treatment by government authorities, not constraints on individual freedoms and the unrepresentative character of government. The most common identifiable "ideology" motivating Chinese behavior, other than economic self-interest, will probably remain a state-centered form of patriotic nationalism. Hence, both the elite and the public will likely continue to favor a strong, authoritarian central government that is able to maintain an emphasis on economic development, preserve social order, and elicit greater respect and authority in the international arena.

Second, despite growing nationalistic sentiments, China's current foreign policy, marked by overall caution and pragmatism, a recognition of the need for a placid regional environment to permit a continued emphasis on economic reform, and a balancing of both cooperation and competition with the West, will also likely continue over the next 10–15 years. In other words, worst-case foreign policy scenarios—associated with a highly aggressive and anti-Western China or a highly unstable, fragmented China—although possible, will probably not result from existing *domestic* trends.

Third, such policy continuity will nonetheless pose significant challenges to U.S. interests in Asia, deriving primarily from the regional anxieties produced by China's continued economic growth and military modernization. Yet such challenges should prove manageable over the next 10–15 years, especially if the United States and key Asian countries actively encourage greater Chinese communication and cooperation internationally and avoid actions that could lead to extreme negative shifts in Chinese domestic political, social, and economic trends. Far less manageable forms of Chinese foreign policy of the type mentioned above could emerge from such shifts, the most serious deriving from various types of military intervention associated with ultraconservative nationalistic views.

Fourth, major shifts in Chinese economic behavior in particular could contribute greatly to the emergence of severely adverse domestic and foreign policy outcomes. Both significant setbacks in the reform effort leading to a severe downturn of the Chinese economy and sustained, very high rates of economic growth and increased central government revenues resulting from the resolution of major reform problems could exacerbate Chinese domestic political and social tensions and increase the likelihood of highly erratic or provocative forms of Chinese external behavior. Thus, a *moderate* level of success in China's economic reforms is in the best interest of both the United States and China.

Fifth, modest and steady increases in China's military budget are also, on balance, in the best interest of the United States, as opposed to either very high (i.e., 10 percent or more) or very low (i.e., 0–5 percent) increases. Such increases are more conducive to Chinese domestic stability and a continuation of China's cautious, relatively cooperative foreign policy stance than either an insufficient or excessive level of military funding. Major (and particularly sudden) leaps in Chinese defense spending, especially on advanced armaments, will greatly increase regional anxieties and could lead to an arms race in Asia. Alternatively, a very low level of government defense spending could produce strong discontent and divisions within the military leadership, leading to domestic political instability or the kinds of military intervention in leadership politics and foreign policy discussed above.

Finally, the above findings suggest several actions that the United States should take (or avoid) to minimize the likelihood of severely adverse Chinese external behavior over the long term.

Strengthen and expand official and unofficial contacts with Chinese civilian and especially military leaders, at both the senior and middle levels. Such contacts are absolutely essential to convey a clearer sense of U.S. interests and intentions toward China and Asia over the long term, and hopefully to weaken the arguments of conservative hardliners within the leadership. These contacts should include frequent discussions with emerging leaders at the national and subnational levels, including members of the Central Committee and National People's Congress, middle- and senior-ranking military officers at both the central and regional levels, leading provincial and municipal officials in both coastal and inland regions, and emerging private or semiprivate business elites. The development of such diverse lines of communication (and especially U.S. links to central military and government officials) should be regarded by Washington as a virtually inviolate element of U.S. policy toward China. In other words, tensions and disputes with Beijing over issues such as trade, human rights, and proliferation should not result in the rupture of such contacts.

Avoid vaguely defined and/or broadly punitive economic or diplomatic actions against China. Such actions could be interpreted by many Chinese leaders as part of a concerted effort to undermine their political and economic system or sow discord within society, and would thus primarily serve to strengthen the hand of hardliners. This would be especially the case if China had not provided a sufficient reason for such U.S. actions (for example, by aggressive behavior toward Taiwan or by clear violations of arms control agreements, etc.). This does not mean that the United States should not apply pressures of any kind against China. U.S. efforts to encourage more open, fair, and predictable Chinese economic practices, to prevent nuclear proliferation, or to promote a greater respect for human rights, for example, might call for a variety of pressures or even sanctions. However, the specific reason, purpose, limits, and desired consequence of any such actions should be defined as clearly as possible in advance and applied in as consistent a manner as possible.

Similarly, avoid insistent public demands designed primarily to bring about fundamental democratic change in China. For example, highly public U.S. demands or pressures for basic political reforms leading to greatly expanded voting rights or the emergence of viable alternative political parties would likely be viewed by both leaders and ordinary citizens as intended to undermine political order and foment social unrest. This would especially be the case during a succession struggle or if a relatively weak, but unified leadership were struggling to consolidate its authority and control in a post-Deng setting. Again, this does not mean that the United States should not continue to encourage a greater respect for human rights and the rule of law, or other changes designed to eliminate various arbitrary, corrupt, and coercive forms of political behavior in China. However, actions intended primarily to alter China's political system should be avoided. The most effective means to encourage China's development toward a more open and cooperative political and social order are indirect, through support for expanded diplomatic, cultural, and people-to-people contacts, continued market-led internal economic development, and economic links with the outside (more on the last point below).

Avoid any U.S. actions that could be viewed as attempts to influence the outcome of a severe leadership succession struggle or to take advantage of China's internal disarray. For example, open support for apparently moderate contenders, direct opposition to perceived hardliners, or broader efforts to obtain certain diplomatic, economic, or military gains during a leadership struggle could easily backfire. Instead, the United States should largely limit its actions in this area to expressions of continued support for a stable and peaceful China and for cooperative relations with whatever leadership emerges. However, the United States should, of course, seek to deter or oppose any aggressive Chinese actions threatening to its interests that emerge as part of the leadership struggle.

Encourage more extensive and durable economic links between China and the United States that promote moderate Chinese growth, and support more general measures that strengthen the overall importance of external economic relations to China's future growth and stability.

Expanded foreign trade, investment, and technology links with China could play a potentially critical role in avoiding the emergence of adverse foreign policy behavior over the long term. Such ties will likely prove essential to the continued vitality of the Chinese economy, given China's increasing demands for investment capital, critical technologies, and product markets. Equally important, a greater reliance on foreign economic ties will serve to strengthen the arguments of moderates and progressives who favor the maintenance of cooperative relations with the West, while weakening the viewpoint of hardliners favoring more autarkic economic policies or the use of foreign economic links to support efforts at coercive diplomacy. This will become particularly important if China succeeds in carrying out major structural reforms that significantly increase the fiscal capabilities of the Chinese government. As indicated above, such a development could encourage more assertive regional policies.

Establish greater coordination and communication on China policy with regional allies and friends, such as Japan, South Korea, Australia, and key ASEAN countries. Such interactions could reduce the regional economic and security anxieties that will probably result from the growth of Chinese economic and military power under the (most likely) "continuity" foreign policy scenario discussed above. It might also help prevent provocative actions by key regional countries under various "discontinuity" foreign policy scenarios that assume considerable domestic Chinese unrest. Moreover, greater regional communication about China could also facilitate a more effective international response in the unlikely event of extreme internal chaos or fragmentation. However, such increased communication will also prove difficult to realize, given the different interests of most of the countries involved, the desire of many countries to maintain a low profile toward China, and the fact that efforts at coordination might be viewed by Beijing as part of a U.S.-led effort to contain China.

Maintain current U.S. military force levels in Japan and South Korea and clarify the division of labor between a power-projection-oriented United States and a primarily defensive-oriented Japanese military. This recommended action should occur as part of a broader effort to restructure and revitalize the U.S.-Japan security relationship. Such an action (the details of which are provided in a companion study cited below) would: (a) impart to Chinese hardliners that the United

States remains committed to continued close relations with its key allies; (b) provide clearer indications, to both mainstream and ultra-conservative Chinese officials, of the extent of future limitations on Japanese military efforts; and (c) reassure other nations that Chinese military modernization will not destabilize the region.

The above suggests that even under a likely "best case" scenario of continuity in the existing features of Chinese foreign policy, the challenges confronting U.S. policy toward China will increase greatly over the coming 10–15 years and beyond. Yet the stakes involved in getting this policy right will also increase proportionately, for both the United States and Asia. Given its rapidly expanding external capabilities and interests, China's future foreign policy stance will play a pivotal role in determining whether the Asian security environment of the future is marked by greater regionwide cooperation, a bipolar division centered on the containment of China, escalating arms races and anarchic power competitions, or other possible midrange configurations. Although this study argues that existing political-military, social, and economic trends within China will probably not lead to extremely adverse Chinese foreign policies (which would contribute greatly to the emergence of the most negative Asian security configurations), it also suggests that domestic factors are only part of the equation. External variables, and especially the actions of the United States, could seriously alter such an assessment. To avoid highly adverse shifts in China's domestic environment and foreign policy, the above general U.S. policy recommendations must be integrated into a broader yet more detailed, well-coordinated and clearly prioritized set of policies designed to simultaneously bring China more fully into the international order and yet also maintain the capability to handle the consequences of the failure of such an effort.[1]

---

[1]Further details on the above policy recommendations and their relation to overall U.S. policy in Asia will be provided in a forthcoming report by Michael D. Swaine and Courtney Purrington. Also see Jonathan Pollack, *Designing a New American Security Strategy for Asia*, Council on Foreign Relations, Asia Project Working Paper (March 1995 expected).

LEADING MEMBERS OF THE PRINCELINGS GROUP

Name of Parent	Name of Child	Relationship	Current Position
Bo Yibo	Bo Xiyong	son	Vice President, China Federation of Automobile Industry
	Bo Xilai	son	Mayor of Dalian, Standing Committee Member, Dalian City Communist Party of China Committee
	Bo Xicheng	son	Director, Beijing Municipality Tourism Bureau
	Zheng Yaowen	son-in-law	Head, African Department, Foreign Affairs Ministry
Chen Yi (deceased)	Chen Haosu	son	Vice President, China People's Association for Friendship with Foreign Countries; former Vice Minister, Radio, Films, and Television
	Chen Danhuai	son	Deputy Commander of a combined arms army
	Chen Xiaolu	son	Chairman, Standard International Corporation
	Chen Xiaoshan	daughter	Department Head, Foreign Affairs Ministry
Chen Yun (deceased)	Chen Yuan	son	Vice President, People's Bank of China
	Chen Weihua	daughter	Deputy Director of a Central Organization Department Unit
Deng Liqun	Deng Yingtao	son	Deputy Director, Chinese Academy of Social Sciences Rural Development Research Institute
Deng Xiaoping	Deng Pufang	son	Executive Director, China Welfare Fund for the Handicapped
	Deng Nan	daughter	Deputy Director, State Science and Technology Commission

	Zhang Hong	Deng Nan's husband	Bureau Director, Chinese Academy of Sciences
	Deng Zhifang	son	Assistant General Manager, China International Trust and Investment Corporation
	Deng Rong	daughter	Secretary to Deng Xiaoping
	He Ping	Deng Rong's husband	Director, Armament Department, People's Liberation Army General Staff Department (He Biao, member of Central Advisory Commission, is his father.)
Gu Mu	Liu Liyuan	son	Divisional Commander, Shenzhen Armed Police Corps, Public Security Ministry
Guo Xiangsheng (deceased)	Guo Shuyan	son	Governor, Hubei Province
He Changgong (deceased)	He Quan	son	Deputy Head of a PLA General Staff Headquarters Department
He Long (deceased)	He Pengfei	son	Rear Admiral, Deputy Commander, Navy
	He Liming	daughter	Former Administrative Department Secretary, Everbright Industrial Corporation
Hu Qiaomu	Hu Shiying	son	Arrested on charges of economic crimes but paroled; present where-abouts unknown
Hu Yaobang (deceased)	Hu Deping	son	Head, Fifth Bureau, CPC Central United Front Work Department
	Liu Hu	son	Former Deputy Bureau Chief, Ministry of Foreign Economic Relations and Trade
Huang Huoqing (deceased)	Huang Chengyi	son	Minister, Energy Resources
Jia Tingsan (deceased)	Jia Chunwang	son	Minister, State Security
Jia Zhenfu (deceased)	Jia Qinglin	son	Governor, Fujian Province
Jiang Nanxiang	Jiang Zhuping	son	Head, Civil Aviation Administration of China
Jiang Shangqing (deceased)	Jiang Zemin	adopted son	General Secretary, CPC Central Committee
Ke Lin (deceased)	Ke Xiaogang	son	Deputy Director, Macao Branch, Xinhua News Agency

Kong Yuan (deceased)	Kong Dan	son	Party Committee Secretary, Hong Kong Everbright Industrial Corporation
Li Fuchun (deceased)	Li Changan	son	Deputy Secretary General, State Council General Office
Li Peng	Li Xiaopeng	son	Engineer, Electricity Research Institute, Ministry of Energy Resources
	Li Xiaoyong	son	Formerly Armed Police Corps Major
	Li Xiaolin	daughter	Engineer, Beijing Power Supply Bureau
Li Weihan (deceased)	Li Tieying	son	Son of Li Weihan and Jin Weiying, Deng Xiaoping's former wife; now State Councillor
	Li Tielian	son	Director, Beijing Municipal Commission for Restructuring the Economy
Liao Chengzhi (deceased)	Liao Hui	son	Director, State Council Overseas Chinese Affairs Office
Lin Biao (deceased)	Lin Liheng	daughter	Working at Chinese Academy of Social Sciences History Department
	Li Hanxiong	nephew	Former Construction Minister, dismissed in 1991; present position unknown
Lin Boqu (deceased)	Lin Yongsan	son	Vice Chairman, Inner Mongolian Autonomous Region
Liu Shaoqi (deceased)	Liu Pingping	daughter	Director, China Food Research Institute (present name Wang Qing)
	Liu Yuanyuan	daughter	Vice Governor, Henan Province (present name Liu Yuan)
	Liu Weiming	nephew	Vice Governor, Guangdong Province
Liu Zhidan (deceased)	Liu Lizhen	son	Vice Chairman, Standing Committee, Shaanxi Provincial People's Congress
Luo Ruiqing (deceased)	Luo Yuping	daughter	Person-in-Charge, Outpatient Section, PLA General Staff Headquarters Medical Department
Mao Zedong (deceased)	Shao Hua	daughter-in-law	Chinese People's Political Consultative Conference
	Wang Hairong	niece	Deputy Director, Councillor's Office, State Council
Ngapoi Ngawang Jigme	Tudao Doje	son	Vice Chairman, Tibet Autonomous Regional People's Government
	Danzim Jigme	son	Major, Tibet Military District

	Jinyuan	son	Office Director, Beijing Foundation for Aid to Tibet
Nie Rongzhen	Nie Li	daughter	Lieutenant General (retired)
	Ding Henggao	son-in-law	Lieutenant General; Director, Commission for Science, Technology, and Industry for National Defense
Peng Pai (deceased)	Peng Shilu	son	Assistant General Manager, China State Shipbuilding Corporation
Peng Zhen	Fu Rui	son	Standing Committee Member, and Organization Department Head, Guangdong Provincial CPC Committee
	Fu Yang	son	Person-in-Charge, Beijing law firm
	Fu Liang	son	Cadre, a foreign-capital firm
	Fu Yan	daughter	Manager, a foreign-capital firm
Qiao Guanhua (deceased)	Qiao Zonghuai	son	PRC Ambassador to Finland
Qin Jiwei	Qin Tian	son	PLA Army- or Divisional-Level cadre
Tao Zhu (deceased)	Tao Siliang	daughter	Head, Sixth Bureau, CPC Central United Front Work Department
Ulanhu (deceased)	Buhe	son	Deputy Secretary, Inner Mongolia Autonomous Region CPC Committee; Chairman, Regional Government
	Zhu Lan Qi Qi Ke	Buhe's wife	Deputy Chief, Inner Mongolian Broadcasting Bureau
	Wu Keli	son	Assistant General Manager, Great Wall Industrial Corporation
	Wu Jie	son	Vice Governor, Shanxi Province
	Yun Shufen	niece	Vice Chairman, Inner Mongolia Autonomous Region CPPCC Committee
	Yun Zhaoguang	nephew	Vice Chairman, Inner Mongolia Autonomous Region CPPCC Committee
Wan Li	Wan Boao	son	Head, International Department, State Physical Culture and Sports Commission
	Wan Zhongxiang	son	Manager of Public Relations, CITIC
	Wan Jifei	son	Deputy Director, Beijing Municipal Commission of Foreign Economic Relations and Trade
Wang Bingqian	Wang Fei	son	Director, Shanxi Province Economic Commission

Wang Jinmei (deceased)	Wang Naien	son	Party Committee Secretary, Shanghai Municipal Traffic Commission
	Wang Naizheng	son	Deputy Commander, Jilin Province Military District
Wang Yifei (deceased)	Wang Jiguang	son	Researcher, State Council International Studies Center
Wang Zhen (deceased)	Wang Bing	son	Ministry of Aeronautics and Astronautics
	Wang Zhi	son	General Manager, Great Wall Computer Group
	Wang Jun		Chairman, CITIC
	He Jingzhi	son-in-law	Acting Cultural Minister
Xi Zhongxun	Xi Jinping	son	Secretary, Fuzhou City CPC Committee
	Xi Jinning	son	Deputy Head, Organization Department, Shaanxi Provincial CPC Committee
Xiao Jingguang	Xiao Congci	son	Secretary, Shanxi Provincial CPC Committee
Yan Baohang (deceased)	Yan Mingfu	son	Vice Minister, Civil Affairs
Yang Shangkun	Yang Shaojing	son	Director of a research institute, COSTIND
	Yang Shaoming	son	Deputy Director, Central Party Literature Research Center
	Yang Li	daughter	CITIC
	Wang Xiaochao	son-in-law	Former Poly Incorporated Manager; now studying in Britain
Yao Yilin	Yao Mingwei	son	Head, International Cooperation Department, Ministry of Machine-Building and Electronics
	Wang Qishan	son-in-law	Vice President, China Construction Bank
Ye Jianying (deceased)	Ye Xuanping	son	Vice Chairman, CPPCC
	Ye Xuanning	son	Head, Liaison Department, PLA General Staff Headquarters
	Ye Chumei	daughter	Deputy Director, Science and Technology Committee, COSTIND
	Wu Xiaolan	daughter-in-law	Ye Xuanping's wife; Vice Chairman, Standing Committee, Shenzhen City People's Congress
	Zou Jiahua	son-in-law	Vice Premier, State Council
Ye Ting (deceased)	Ye Zhengming	son	Director, Shenzhen Science and Technology Commission

	Ye Zhengda	son	Lieutenant General; Deputy Director, Science and Technology Committee, COSTIND
	Ye Huaming	son	President, Shenzhen Advanced-Science Laser Company
Yu Wen	Sun Xiaoyu	son	Deputy Director, State Council Office of Taiwan Affairs
Zeng Shan (deceased)	Zeng Qinghong	son	Deputy Director, CPC Central Committee General Office
	Wu Shaozu	son-in-law	Director, State Physical Culture and Sports Commission
Zhang Aiping	Yu Zhengsheng	son-in-law	Mayor of Qingdao; Deputy Secretary, Qingdao City CPC Committee
	Zhang Pin	son	Deputy Director, Foreign Affairs Bureau, COSTIND
	Zhang Zhikai	daughter	Director, Yantai City Economic Commission
Zhao Ziyang	Zhao Nansheng	daughter	Public Relations Manager, Beijing Great Wall Hotel
Zhou Enlai (deceased)	Li Peng	adopted son	Premier, State Council
	Peng Shilu	adopted son	Assistant General Manager, China State Shipbuilding Corporation
Zhu De (deceased)	Zhu Min	daughter	Head, Foreign Language Department, Beijing Normal University
Zou Taofen (deceased)	Zou Jiahua	son	Vice Premier, State Council

SOURCE: Adapted from "Conditions of Present, Previous CPC Leaders' Children," *Tangtai* (Hong Kong), April 15, 1992, pp. 53–58, reproduced in *JPRS-China*, May 13, 1992, pp. 4–9, and with subsequent updating from U.S. government sources.

BIBLIOGRAPHY

Alford, William P., "Double-Edged Swords Cut Both Ways: Law and Legitimacy in the People's Republic of China," *Daedalus*, Vol. 122, No. 2, Spring 1993, pp. 45–69.

"Army Paper Discusses Jiang's Military Ties," *Kyodo News Service*, August 2, 1993, in *FBIS-CHI*, August 2, 1993, p. 23.

Ash, Robert F., and Y. Y. Kueh, "Economic Integration Within Greater China: Trade and Investment Flows Between China, Hong Kong, and Taiwan," *China Quarterly*, No. 136, December 1993, pp. 711–745.

Ashton, William, "Chinese Naval Base: Many Rumors, Few Facts," *Asia-Pacific Defense Reporter*, Vol. 19/20, No. 12/1, June–July 1993, p. 25.

Bachman, David, "The Limits to Leadership in China," in "The Future of China," *NBR Analysis*, Vol. 3, No. 3, August 1992, pp. 23–35.

Bachman, David, "The Fourteenth Congress of the Chinese Communist Party," *Asian Update*, The Asia Society, New York, November 1992.

Bachman, David, "Domestic Sources of Chinese Foreign Policy," in Samuel Kim (ed.), *China and the World: Chinese Foreign Relations in the Post–Cold War Era*, Westview Press, Boulder, Colorado, 1994.

Barnett, A. Doak, *The Making of Foreign Policy in China: Structure and Process*, Westview Press, Boulder, 1985.

Baum, Julian, Tai Ming Cheung, and Lincoln Kaye, "Ancient Fears," *Far Eastern Economic Review*, December 3, 1992, pp. 8–10.

Baum, Richard, "The China Syndrome: Prospects for Democracy in the Middle Kingdom," *Harvard International Review*, Vol. 15, No. 2, Winter 1992/93, pp. 32–33, 66.

Bert, Wayne, "Chinese Policies and U.S. Interests in Southeast Asia," *Asian Survey*, Vol. 33, No. 3, March 1993, pp. 317–332.

Bickford, Thomas J., "The Chinese Military and Its Business Operations," *Asian Survey*, Vol. 34, No. 5, May 1995, pp. 460–474.

Bitzinger, Richard A., "Arms to Go: Chinese Arms Sales to the Third World," *International Security*, Vol. 17, No. 2, Fall 1992, pp. 84–111.

Branigin, William, "As China Builds Arsenal and Bases, Asians Wary of 'Rogue in the Region'," *Washington Post*, March 31, 1993, pp. A-21, A-27.

Brick, Andrew, "Borderless Economics Forces Change in China," *Asian Wall Street Journal*, October 15, 1992, p. 10.

Central Intelligence Agency, *China's Economy in 1992 and 1993, Grappling with the Risks of Rapid Growth*, Directorate of Intelligence, Washington, D.C., August 1993.

Chan, Anita, "Revolution or Corporatism?   Workers and Trade Unions in Post-Mao China," *Australian Journal of Chinese Affairs*, No. 29, January 1993, pp. 31–61.

Chanda, Nayan, and Lincoln Kaye, "Circling Hawks," *Far Eastern Economic Review*, October 7, 1993, pp. 12–13.

Chang Hua, "CPC Document No. 4 Changes Slogan, Stressing Main Role of Market Regulation," *Ching Chi Jih Pao* (Hong Kong), June 4, 1992, p. 8, in *FBIS-CHI*, June 4, 1992, p. 21.

Chang, Parris H., "Beijing's Relations with Taiwan," in Parris H. Chang and Martin Lasater (eds.), *If China Crosses the Taiwan Strait: The International Response*, University Press of America, New York, 1993,   pp. 1–13.

Chang Ya-chün, "Peking's Asia-Pacific Strategy in the 1990's," *Issues and Studies*, January 1993, pp. 75–98.

"The Changing Roles of the Village Party Secretary," *China News Analysis*, No. 1488, July 1, 1993.

Chen, Kathy, and Joseph Kahn, "Nervous Beijing Backtracks on Speedy Economic Reform," *Asian Wall Street Journal*, April 7–8, 1995.

Chen Qimao, "New Approaches in China's Foreign Policy: The Post–Cold War Era," *Asian Survey*, Vol. 33, No. 3, March 1993, pp. 237–251.

Chen Te-sheng, "Mainland China's Economic Prospects in View of the Five-and Ten-Year Economic Plans," *Issues and Studies*, Vol. 27, No. 8, August 1991, pp. 71–81.

Chen Yizi, "Problems of Communism and Changes in China," *Journal of Contemporary China*, Vol. 2, No. 1, Winter–Spring 1993, pp. 82–86.

Cheng Tiejun, "China's Peasants and Democracy," *Asian Wall Street Journal*, March 29, 1993, p. 12.

Cheung, Tai Ming, "Loaded Weapons: China on Arms Buying Spree in Former Soviet Union," *Far Eastern Economic Review*, September 3, 1992, p. 21.

Cheung, Tai Ming, "Who's on Top? China's Military Faces a Leadership Vacuum," *Far Eastern Economic Review*, April 22, 1993, p. 18.

Cheung, Tai Ming, "Making Money, Not War," *China Trade Report*, August 1993, pp. 5–6.

Cheung, Tai Ming, "Elusive Ploughshares," *Far Eastern Economic Review*, October 14, 1993, pp. 70–71.

Cheung, Tai Ming, "Serve the People," *Far Eastern Economic Review*, October 14, 1993, pp. 64–66.

Cheung, Tai Ming, "Profits over Professionalism: The PLA's Economic Activities and the Impact on Military Unity," in Richard

H. Yang et al. (eds.), *Chinese Regionalism: The Security Dimension*, Westview, Boulder, Colorado, 1994, pp. 85–110.

Clarke, Christopher M., "China's Transition to the Post-Deng Era," in *China's Economic Dilemmas in the 1990's: The Problems of Reforms, Modernization, and Interdependence*, study papers submitted to the Joint Economic Committee, Congress of the United States, U.S. Government Printing Office, Washington, D.C., 1991, pp. 1–14.

"Conditions of Present, Previous CPC Leaders' Children," *Tangtai* (Hong Kong), April 15, 1992, pp. 53–58, in *JPRS-China*, May 13, 1992, pp. 4–9.

"The CPC Issues Document Number Four, Fully Expounding Expansion of Opening Up," *Ta Kung Pao* (Hong Kong), June 18, 1992, p. 2, in *FBIS-CHI*, June 18, 1992, pp. 19–20.

Delfs, Robert, "Zhao Ziyang in the Shadows: Prospects for Party Liberals in the Succession Struggle After Deng Xiaoping," paper prepared for the Fifth Annual Staunton Hill Conference on the People's Liberation Army, June 17–19, 1994.

Ding, Arthur S., "The Nature and Impact of the PLA's Business Activities," *Issues and Studies*, August, 1993, pp. 85–100.

Dittmer, Lowell, "Bases of Power in Chinese Politics: A Theory and an Analysis of the Fall of the 'Gang of Four,'" *World Politics*, Vol. 31, No. 1, October 1978, pp. 26–60.

Dittmer, Lowell, and Samuel S. Kim (eds.), *China's Quest for National Identity*, Cornell University Press, Ithaca and London, 1993.

Ebanks, G. Edward, and Chaoze Cheng, "China: A Unique Urbanization Model," *Asia-Pacific Population Journal*, Vol. 5, No. 3, 1990, pp. 29–50.

Eberstadt, Nicholas, "Population Change and National Security," *Foreign Affairs*, Vol. 70, No. 3, 1991, pp. 115–131.

The Economist Intelligence Unit, *Country Report, 1st Quarter 1994, China Mongolia*, New York, 1994.

"The Eighth NPC and the State of the Nation," *China News Analysis*, No. 1484, May 1, 1993.

An Eye on China, No. 10, Kim Eng Securities, Hong Kong, January 1995.

Fewsmith, Joseph, "Neoconservatism and the End of the Dengist Era," unpublished paper presented at a UCLA-sponsored conference on "China After Deng," held March 11, 1995.

"The Fourteenth Party Congress: In Session," *China News Analysis*, No. 1471, November 1, 1992.

Friedman, Edward, "A Failed Chinese Modernity," *Daedalus*, Vol. 122, No. 2, Spring 1993, pp. 1–17.

"Further Price Reforms," *China News Analysis*, No. 1472, November 15, 1992.

Garnaut, Ross, and Liu Guoguang (eds.), *Economic Reform and Internationalisation: China and the Pacific Region*, Allen & Unwin, Paul & Co. Pubs., Concord, Massachusetts, 1992.

Garver, John W., "China's Push Through the South China Sea: The Interaction of Bureaucratic and National Interests," *China Quarterly*, No. 132, December 1992, pp. 999–1028.

Gill, R. Bates, " The Challenge of Chinese Arms Proliferation," paper presented at the Fourth Annual Staunton Hill Conference on the People's Liberation Army, August 27–29, 1993.

Glaser, Bonnie S., "China's Security Perceptions: Interests and Ambitions," *Asian Survey*, Vol. 33, No. 3, March 1993, pp. 252–271.

Godwin, Paul H. B., "Changing Concepts of Doctrine, Strategy, and Operations in the People's Liberation Army 1978–87," *The China Quarterly*, No. 112, December 1987, pp. 573–590.

Goldman, Merle, Perry Link, and Su Wei, "China's Intellectuals in the Deng Era: Loss of Identity with the State," in Lowell Dittmer and Samuel S. Kim (eds.), *China's Quest for National Identity*, Cornell University Press, Ithaca and London, 1993, pp. 125–153.

Goodman, David, et al., *Southern China in Transition: The New Regionalism and Australia*, East Asia Analytical Unit, Canberra, 1992.

Gottschang, Thomas R., "The Economy's Continued Growth," *Current History*, Vol. 91, No. 566, September 1992, pp. 268–272.

Hamrin, Carol Lee, *China and the Challenge of the Future: Changing Political Patterns*, Westview Press, Boulder, Colorado, 1990.

Hamrin, Carol Lee, "The Party Leadership System," in Kenneth G. Lieberthal and David M. Lampton (eds.), *Bureaucracy, Politics, and Decision Making in Post-Mao China*, University of California Press, Berkeley, 1992, pp. 95–124.

Hamrin, Carol Lee, "Elite Politics and the Development of China's Foreign Relations," in Thomas W. Robinson and David Shambaugh (eds.), *Chinese Foreign Policy: Theory and Practice*, Clarendon Press, Oxford, 1994, pp. 70–112.

Hao, Jia, and Lin Zhimin (eds.), *Changing Central-Local Relations in China*, Westview Press, Boulder, Colorado, 1994.

Harding, Harry, *China's Second Revolution: Reform After Mao*, The Brookings Institution, Washington, D.C., 1987.

Harding, Harry, "The Role of the Military in Chinese Politics," in Victor Falkenheim (ed.), *Citizens and Groups in Contemporary China*, Center for Chinese Studies, University of Michigan, Ann Arbor, 1987, pp. 213–256.

He Pin, "Jiang Zemin Seeks to Strengthen His Personal Military Power," *China Focus*, Vol. 2, No. 2, February 1, 1994, pp. 1, 5.

Hiraiwa, Kozue, "Foreign Investment in the PRC, 1990–1991," *JETRO China Newsletter*, No. 96, January–February 1992, pp. 11–21.

Ho Chin-ming, "China: The 31 Military Power Holders," *Jane's Intelligence Review*, Vol. 3, No. 9, September 1991, pp. 424–427.

Holley, David, "China Moves to Entrench New Generation of Leaders," *Los Angeles Times*, March 28, 1993.

Holley, David, "China's Hard-Line Premier Wins 2nd Term," *Los Angeles Times*, March 29, 1993.

Holley, David, "Power in Beijing Finally Flowing to Younger Generation," *Los Angeles Times*, April 2, 1993, p. A-8.

Hsia, Hsiao-tan, "People's Armed Police Force Is Placed Again Under Command of Central Military Commission, and the Force Is Facing High-Level Leadership Changes," *Ming Pao* (Hong Kong), June 16, 1993, p. 8, in *FBIS-CHI*, June 18, 1993, pp. 27–28.

Hu, Weixing, "Beijing's New Thinking on Security Strategy," *The Journal of Contemporary China*, No. 3, Summer 1993, pp. 50–65.

Hua Di, "Ballistic Missile Exports Will Continue," *Asia-Pacific Defence Reporter*, Vol. 18, No. 3, September 1991, pp. 14–15.

Huang Yasheng, "Central-Local Relations in China During the Reform Era: The Economic and Institutional Dimensions," unpublished paper presented at a UCLA-sponsored conference on "China After Deng," held March 11, 1995.

Hunt, Michael H., "Chinese National Identity and the Strong State: The Late Qing-Republican Crisis," in Lowell Dittmer and Samuel S. Kim (eds.), *China's Quest for National Identity*, Cornell University Press, Ithaca and London, 1993, pp. 62–79.

Imai, Satoshi, "The Structure of Trade in China—Changes and Factors," *JETRO China Newsletter*, No. 101, November–December, 1992, pp. 20–24.

International Monetary Fund, *World Economic Outlook*, Washington, D.C., October 1993.

Jencks, Harlan W., *From Muskets to Missiles: Politics and Professionalism in the Chinese Army, 1945–1981*, Westview Press, Boulder, Colorado, 1982.

Jia Hao and Lin Zhimin, *Changing Central-Local Relations in China: Reform and State Capacity*, Westview Press, Boulder, Colorado, 1994.

Joffe, Ellis, "China's Military: The PLA in Internal Politics," *Problems of Communism*, Vol. 24, November/December 1975, pp. 1–12.

Johnson, Alastair I., "Changing Party-Army Relations in China, 1979–1984," *Asian Survey*, Vol. 24, No. 10, October 1984, pp. 1012–1039.

Kan, Shirley A., *Chinese Missile and Nuclear Proliferation: Issues for Congress*, Congressional Research Service, Library of Congress, Washington D.C., September 1, 1993.

Kao Charng, "A 'Greater China Economic Sphere': Reality and Prospects," *Issues and Studies*, Vol. 28, No. 11, November 1992, pp. 49–64.

Kaye, Lincoln, "Back in the Game," *Far Eastern Economic Review*, June 11, 1992, p. 9.

Kaye, Lincoln, "Uncertain Patrimony," *Far Eastern Economic Review*, October 29, 1992, pp. 10–12.

Kaye, Lincoln, "Broad Canvass," *Far Eastern Economic Review*, October 29, 1992, pp. 12–13.

Kaye, Lincoln, "Back to the Front," *Far Eastern Economic Review*, October 29, 1992, pp. 15–16.

Kelliher, Daniel, "Keeping Democracy Safe from the Masses: Intellectuals and Elitism in the Chinese Protest Movement," *Comparative Politics*, Vol. 25, No. 4, July 1993, pp. 379–396.

Kim, Samuel S., "China as a Regional Power," *Current History*, Vol. 91, No. 566, September 1992, pp. 247–252.

Kim, Samuel S. (ed.), *China and the World: Chinese Foreign Relations in the Post–Cold War Era*, Westview Press, Boulder, Colorado, 1994.

Kirby, William C., "Traditions of Centrality, Authority, and Management in Modern China's Foreign Relations," in Thomas W. Robinson and David Shambaugh (eds.), *Chinese Foreign Policy: Theory and Practice*, Clarendon Press, Oxford, 1994, pp. 13–29.

Kristof, Nicholas, "China Builds Its Military Muscle, Making Some Neighbors Nervous," *New York Times*, January 11, 1993, pp. 1, 4.

Lam, Willy Wo-lap, "Conservatives Reportedly Restrict Document No. 4," *South China Morning Post*, June 27, 1992, p. 9, in *FBIS-CHI*, June 29, 1992, pp. 18–19.

Lam, Willy Wo-lap, "Beijing Said to Crack Down on Army, Police Corruption," *South China Morning Post*, September 10, 1993, p. 8, in *FBIS-CHI*, September 10, 1993, pp. 35–36.

Lam, Willy Wo-lap, "Military 'Reshuffle' Said Planned for 'Late November," *South China Morning Post*, October 21, 1993, p. 1, in *FBIS-CHI*, October 21, 1993, pp. 30–31.

Lampton, David M., *Paths to Power: Elite Mobility in Contemporary China*, Center for Chinese Studies, University of Michigan, Ann Arbor, 1989.

Lampton, David M., "China's Biggest Problem: Gridlock, Not Revolution," in *China's Economic Dilemmas in the 1990's: The Problems of Reforms, Modernization, and Interdependence*, study papers submitted to the Joint Economic Committee, Congress of the United States, U.S. Government Printing Office, Washington, D.C., 1991, pp. 65–69.

Lampton, David M., "China and the Strategic Quadrangle: Foreign Policy Continuity in an Age of Discontinuity," in Michael Mandelbaum (ed.), *The Strategic Quadrangle: Japan, China, Russia, and the United States in East Asia*, Council on Foreign Relations Press, New York, 1994.

Lardy, Nicholas R., "China's Growing Economic Role in Asia," in "The Future of China," *NBR Analysis*, Vol. 3, No. 3, August 1992, pp. 5–12.

Lardy, Nicholas R., *China in the World Economy*, Institute for International Economics, Washington, D.C., 1994.

Latham, Richard J., and Kenneth W. Allen, "Defense Reform in China: The PLA Air Force," *Problems of Communism*, Vol. 40, May–June 1991, pp. 30–50.

Lee, Hong Yung, "Leadership Trend Emerges in China: Pragmatists Replacing China's Old Revolutionaries," *Asia-Pacific Briefing Paper*, No. 2, East-West Center, Honolulu, May 1991.

Lee Lai To, "ASEAN-PRC Political and Security Cooperation: Problems, Proposals, and Prospects," *Asian Survey*, Vol. 33, No. 11, November 1993, pp. 1095–1104.

Leung, Julia, "China Faces Growing Economic Polarity," *Asian Wall Street Journal*, July 30, 1991, pp. 1, 7.

Levine, Steven I., "China and America: The Resilient Relationship," *Current History*, Vol. 91, No. 566, September 1992, pp. 241–246.

Lewis, John W., and Hua Di, "China's Ballistic Missile Programs," *International Security*, Vol. 17, No. 2, Fall 1992, pp. 5–40.

Lewis, John W., Hua Di, and Xue Litai, "Beijing's Defense Establishment: Solving the Arms-Export Enigma," *International Security*, Vol. 15, No. 4, Spring 1991, pp. 87–109.

Li Cheng and David Bachman, "Localism, Elitism, and Immobilism: Elite Formation and Social Change in Post-Mao China," *World Politics*, Vol. 42, No. 1, October 1989, pp. 64–94.

Li Cheng and Lynn White, "The Thirteenth Central Committee of the Chinese Communist Party: From Mobilizers to Managers," *Asian Survey*, Vol. 28, No. 4, April 1988, pp. 371–399.

Li Cheng and Lynn White, "Elite Transformation and Modern Change in Mainland China and Taiwan: Empirical Data and the Theory of Technocracy," *China Quarterly*, No. 121, March 1990, pp. 1–35.

Li Cheng and Lynn White, "The Army in the Succession to Deng Xiaoping: Familiar Fealties and Technocratic Trends," *Asian Survey*, Vol. 33, No. 8, August 1993, pp. 757–786.

Lieberthal, Kenneth G., "The Dynamics of Internal Policies," in *China's Economic Dilemmas in the 1990's: The Problems of Reforms, Modernization, and Interdependence*, study papers submitted to the Joint Economic Committee, Congress of the United States, U.S. Government Printing Office, Washington, D.C., 1991, pp. 15–28.

Lieberthal, Kenneth G., "China in the Year 2000: Politics and International Security," in "The Future of China," *NBR Analysis*, Vol. 3, No. 3, August 1992, pp. 13–22.

Lieberthal, Kenneth G., and Michael Lampton (eds.), *Bureaucracy, Politics, and Decision Making in Post-Mao China*, University of California Press, Berkeley, 1992, pp. 245–279.

Lilley, James, "An American View: U.S. Relations with the PRC and Taiwan," *Journal of Northeast Asian Studies*, Fall 1992, pp. 84–89.

Lin, Chong-Pin, "The People's Liberation Army and the Fourteenth Party Congress of the Chinese Communist Party," paper presented to the Fourth Annual Staunton Hill Conference on the People's Liberation Army, August 27–29, 1993.

Lin Tongqi, "A Search for China's Soul," *Daedalus*, Vol. 122, No. 2, Spring 1993, pp. 171–188.

Link, Perry, "China's Core Problem," *Daedalus*, Vol. 122, No. 2, Spring 1993, pp. 189–205.

Lo Ping and Li Tzu-ching, "Jiang Zemin Enhances Political Standing of the Generals, Now Numbering 10," *Cheng Ming* (Hong Kong), September 1, 1993, pp. 12–13, in *FBIS-CHI*, September 7, 1993, pp. 46–48.

Luo Qi and Christopher Howe, "Direct Investment and Economic Integration in the Asia-Pacific: The Case of Taiwanese Investment in Xiamen," *China Quarterly*, 1993, pp. 747–769.

Lu Yu-shan, "CPC Prohibits Armed Forces from Engaging in Business," *Tangtai* (Hong Kong), No. 35, February 15, 1994, pp. 14–15, in FBIS-CHI, February 7, 1994, pp. 23–24.

Mainichi Shimbun, April 15, 1991, p. 7, reprinted in *FBIS, Daily Report—People's Republic of China*, April 16, 1991, Annex, p. 2.

Maruya, Toyojiro, "The Development of the Guangdong Economy and Its Ties with Beijing," *JETRO China Newsletter*, No. 96, January–February 1992, pp. 2–10.

McCormick, Barrett L., "Democracy or Dictatorship? A Response to Gordon White," *Australian Journal of Chinese Affairs*, No. 31, January 1994, pp. 95–110.

McKinnon, Ronald I., "China's Tentative Freedoms," *Asian Wall Street Journal*, February 23, 1994, p. 6.

McNamara, Robert S., et al., *Sino-American Military Relations: Mutual Responsibilities in the Post-Cold War Era*, National Committee China Policy Series, No. Nine, New York, November 1994.

The Military Balance 1993–1994, The International Institute for Strategic Studies, London, 1993.

Miller, H. Lyman, "The Post-Deng Leadership: Premature Reports of Demise?" *Washington Journal of Modern China*, Vol. 2, No. 2, Fall/Winter 1994, pp. 1–16.

Mills, William deB., "Generational Change in China," *Problems of Communism*, Vol. 32, No. 6, November–December 1983.

Morgan, T. Clifton, "Economic Ties, Influence, and Taiwan-Mainland China Relations," *Issues and Studies*, Vol. 29, No. 3, March 1993, pp. 1–14.

Nan Li, "War Doctrine, Strategic Principles and Operational Concepts of the People's Liberation Army: New Developments (1985–1993)," unpublished paper, Olin Institute, Harvard University, Cambridge, Massachusetts, pp. 7–14.

Nathan, Andrew, "Tiananmen and the Cosmos," *The New Republic*, July 29, 1991, Vol. 205, No. 5, pp. 31–36.

Nathan, Andrew, "Chinese Democracy: The Lessons of Failure," *The Journal of Contemporary China*, No. 4, Fall 1993, pp. 3-13.

Nathan, Andrew, and Tianjin Shi, "Cultural Requisites for Democracy in China: Findings from a Survey," *Daedalus*, Vol. 122, No. 2, Spring 1993, pp. 95–123.

Naughton, Barry, "Hierarchy and the Bargaining Economy: Government and Enterprise in the Reform Process," in Kenneth G. Lieberthal and Michael Lampton (eds.), *Bureaucracy, Politics, and*

Decision Making in Post-Mao China, University of California Press, Berkeley, 1992, pp. 245–279.

Naughton, Barry, "The Foreign Policy Implications of China's Economic Development Strategy," in Thomas W. Robinson and David Shambaugh (eds.), *Chinese Foreign Policy: Theory and Practice*, Clarendon Press, Oxford, 1994, pp. 47–69.

Oksenberg, Michel, "China's Confident Nationalism," *Foreign Affairs*, Winter 1986–87, pp. 501–523.

Oksenberg, Michel, "The China Problem," *Foreign Affairs*, Vol. 70, No. 3, 1991, pp. 1–16.

Oksenberg, Michel, and Kenneth Lieberthal, *Policy Making in China: Leaders, Structures, and Processes*, Princeton University Press, Princeton, 1988.

Overholt, William H., *The Rise of China: How Economic Reform Is Creating a New Superpower*, W. W. Norton and Company, New York, 1993.

Pan Shiying, *Reflections on Modern Strategy: Post Cold War Strategic Theory*, Shijie Zhishi Chubanshe, Beijing, 1993.

"The People's Armed Police," *China News Analysis*, No. 1482, April 1, 1993.

Pernia, Ernesto M., *Urbanization, Population Distribution and Economic Development in Asia*, Asian Development Bank, Economics and Development Resource Center, February 1993, p. 9.

Pollack, Jonathan D., "China and Asia's Nuclear Future," in Francine Frankel (ed.), *Bridging the Nonproliferation Divide: The United States and India*, the University Press of America, Lanham, Maryland, 1995, pp. 98–119.

Pollack, Jonathan D., *Designing a New American Security Strategy for Asia*, Council on Foreign Relations, Asia Project Working Paper (March 1995 expected).

"The Price of Economic Reforms: Central-Local Tensions," *China News Analysis*, No. 1508, April 15, 1994.

"Problems Facing the 'New' Chinese Administration," *JETRO China Newsletter*, No. 105, July–August 1993, pp. 11–24.

Pye, Lucian, "China: Erratic State, Frustrated Society," *Foreign Affairs*, Vol. 69, No. 4, Fall 1990, pp. 56–74.

Pye, Lucian, "How China's Nationalism Was Shanghaied," *Australian Journal of Chinese Affairs*, No. 29, January 1993, pp. 107–133.

Qin Shijun, "High Tech Industrialization in China: An Analysis of the Current Status," *Asian Survey*, Vol. 32, No. 12, December 1992.

"Regional Commander Slated for Removal," *Kyodo News Service*, October 25, 1993, in *FBIS-CHI*, October 26, 1993, p. 20.

Robinson, Thomas W., and David Shambaugh (eds.), *Chinese Foreign Policy: Theory and Practice*, Clarendon Press, Oxford, 1994.

Segal, Gerald, "The PLA and Chinese Foreign Policy Decision-Making," *International Affairs*, Vol. 57, No. 3, Summer 1981, pp. 449–466.

Shambaugh, David, "China's Security Strategy in the Post–Cold War Era," *Survival*, Vol. 34, No. 2, Summer 1992, pp. 88–106.

Shambaugh, David, "Regaining Political Momentum: Deng Strikes Back," *Current History*, Vol. 91, No. 566, September 1992, pp. 257–261.

Shambaugh, David, "Growing Strong: China's Challenge to Asian Security," paper presented to the Fourth Annual Staunton Hill Conference on the People's Liberation Army, August 27–29, 1993.

Shambaugh, David, "Losing Control: The Erosion of State Authority in China," *Current History*, Vol. 92, September 1993, pp. 253–259.

Shambaugh, David, "Introduction, The Emergence of 'Greater China,'" *China Quarterly*, No. 136, December 1993, pp. 653–659.

Shambaugh, David, "China's Commander-in-Chief: Jiang Zemin and the PLA," paper prepared for the Sixth Annual AEI Conference on the People's Liberation Army, June 1995.

Shirk, Susan, "'Playing to the Provinces': Deng Xiaoping's Political Strategy of Economic Reform," *Studies in Comparative Communism*, Vol. 23, No. 3/4, Autumn/Winter 1990, pp. 227–258.

Shirk, Susan, *The Political Logic of Economic Reform in China*, University of California Press, Berkeley, 1993.

Siu, Helen, "Cultural Identity and the Politics of Difference in South China," *Daedalus*, Vol. 122, No. 2, Spring 1993, pp. 19–43.

"Social Security: The Unemployed and Retired," *China News Analysis*, No. 1502, January 15, 1994.

Song, Yann-Huei (Billy), "China and the Military Use of the Ocean," *Ocean Development and International Law*, Vol. 20, 1989, pp. 213–235.

"Strong Chinese Economy Brings New Records in Sino-Japanese Trade," *JETRO China Newsletter*, No. 103, March–April 1993, pp. 22–24.

Sugimoto, Takashi, "The Political Stability of Ethnic Regions in China: A Methodological Study," International Institute for Global Peace, Tokyo, April 1993.

Sung, Yun-Wing, "The Economic Integration of Hong Kong, Taiwan, and South Korea with the Mainland of China," in Ross Garnaut and Liu Guoguang (eds.), *Economic Reform and Internationalisation: China and the Pacific Region*, Allen & Unwin, Paul & Co. Pubs., Concord, Massachusetts, 1992.

"Survey of Residents' 'Tolerance Level' for Reform," *Guanli Shijie* [*Management World*], No. 5, September 24, 1993, pp. 189–198, in *FBIS-CHI*, December 22, 1993.

Sutter, Robert G., Shirley Kan, and Kerry Dumbaugh, "China in Transition: Changing Conditions and Implications for U.S. Interests," *CRS Report for Congress*, Congressional Research Service, Library of Congress, Washington, D.C., December 20, 1993.

Swaine, Michael D., *The Military and Political Succession in China: Leadership, Institutions, Beliefs*, RAND, R-4254-AF, Santa Monica, California, 1992.

Swaine, Michael D., "Chinese Regional Forces as Political Actors," in Richard H. Yang, Jason C. Hu, Peter Kien-hong Yu, and Andrew N. D. Yang (eds.), *Chinese Regionalism: The Security Dimension*, Westview Press, Boulder, Colorado, April 1994.

Swaine, Michael D., "The Modernization of the Chinese People's Liberation Army: Prospects and Implications for Northeast Asia," *NBR Analysis*, Vol. 5, No. 3, October 1994.

Swaine, Michael D., "Leadership Succession in China: Implications for Domestic and Regional Stability," paper prepared for the RAND-Sejong Project on East Asia's Potential for Instability and Crisis, February 1995.

Swaine, Michael D., "Strategic Appraisal: China," in Zalmay Khalilzad (ed.), *Strategic Appraisal 1995*, RAND, forthcoming.

Swaine, Michael D., and Courtney Purrington, with Don Henry, Ashley Tellis, and James Winnefeld, *Asia's Changing Security Environment: Sources of Adversity for U.S. Policy*, RAND, forthcoming.

"Taiwan Politics: Still Muddling, Not Yet Through," *China News Analysis*, No. 1499, December 15, 1993.

Tefft, Sheila, "China's Military Grapples with Conversion," *Christian Science Monitor*, February 7, 1994, p. 4.

Tokyo Colloquium, *Asia: New Challenges and Opportunities*, 1993.

Townsend, James, "Chinese Nationalism," *Australian Journal of Chinese Affairs*, January 1992, pp. 97–130.

Triplett, William C., II, "China's Weapons Mafia," *Washington Post*, October 27, 1991.

Tsang Shu-ki and Cheng Yuk-shing, "China's Tax Reforms of 1994: Breakthrough or Compromise?" *Asian Survey*, Vol. 34, No. 9, September 1994, pp. 769–788.

Tseng Hui-yen, "Jiang Zemin Signs New Lieutenant General Namelist," *Lien Ho Pao* (Hong Kong), October 22, 1993, p. 10, in *FBIS-CHI*, October 22, 1993, pp. 22–23.

Tung, Ricky, "Economic Interaction Between Taiwan and South China's Fukien and Kwangtung Provinces," *Issues and Studies*, Vol. 29, No. 7, pp. 26–42.

Tyson, James L., and Ann Scott Tyson, "Chinese Reforms Widen Gap Between Coast and Hinterland," *Christian Science Monitor*, July 22, 1992, pp. 9–12.

U.S. Arms Control and Disarmament Agency, *World Military Expenditures and Arms Transfers, 1990*, Washington, D.C., 1991.

U.S. Congress, *China's Economic Dilemmas in the 1990's: The Problems of Reforms, Modernization, and Interdependence*, Vol. 1, study papers submitted to the Joint Economic Committee, U.S. Government Printing Office, Washington, D.C., 1991.

Walder, Andrew G., and Gong Xiaoxia, "Workers in the Tiananmen Protests: The Politics of the Beijing Workers' Autonomous Federation," *Australian Journal of Chinese Affairs*, No. 29, January 1993, pp. 1–29.

Wang Chi, "Power Structure and Key Political Players in China," in *China's Economic Dilemmas in the 1990's: The Problems of Reforms, Modernization, and Interdependence*, study papers submitted to the Joint Economic Committee, Congress of the United States, U.S. Government Printing Office, Washington, D.C., 1991, pp. 29–47.

Wang Gungwu, "To Reform a Revolution: Under the Righteous Mandate," *Daedalus*, Vol. 122, No. 2, Spring 1993, pp. 71–94.

Wang Jianwei and Lin Zhimin, "Chinese Perceptions in the Post–Cold War Era: Three Images of the United States," *Asian Survey*, Vol. 32, No. 10, October 1992, pp. 902–917.

Wang Jisi, "International Relations Theory and the Study of Chinese Foreign Policy: A Chinese Perspective," in Thomas W. Robinson and David Shambaugh (eds.), *Chinese Foreign Policy: Theory and Practice*, Clarendon Press, Oxford, 1994, pp. 481–505.

Wang Jisi, "Pragmatic Nationalism: China Seeks a New Role in World Affairs," *Oxford International Review*, Winter 1994.

Wei Li, *The Chinese Staff System*, Institute of East Asian Studies, Berkeley, 1994.

"When China Wakes," *The Economist, A Survey of China*, November 28, 1992.

White, Gordon, "Prospects for Civil Society in China: A Case Study of Xiaoshan City," *Australian Journal of Chinese Affairs*, No. 29, January 1993, pp. 63–87.

White, Gordon, "Democratization and Economic Reform in China," *Australian Journal of Chinese Affairs*, No. 31, January 1994, pp. 73–92.

Whiting, Allen, "Assertive Nationalism in Chinese Foreign Policy," *Asian Survey*, August 1993, pp. 913–933.

Whyte, Martin King, "Prospects for Democratization in China," *Problems of Communism*, Vol. 41, May–June 1992, pp. 58–70.

Wolf, Charles, Jr., et al., *Long-Term Economic and Military Trends, 1950–2010*, RAND, N-2757-USDP, Santa Monica, 1989.

Wong, Christine P. W., "Central-Local Relations in an Era of Fiscal Decline: The Paradox of Fiscal Decentralization in Post-Mao China," *China Quarterly*, No. 128, December 1991, pp. 691–715.

World Bank, *World Development Report 1993*, Washington, D.C.

WuDunn, Sheryl, "Booming China Is a Dream Market for West," *New York Times*, February 15, 1993, pp. A-1, A-6.

WuDunn, Sheryl, "As China Leaps Ahead, the Poor Slip Behind," *New York Times*, May 23, 1993, p. E-3.

Wu Futang, "Jiang Zemin Holds Six Key Posts, and Ba Zhongtan Is Being Transferred to Beijing to Command China's Armed Police Forces," *Kuang Chiao Ching* (Hong Kong), No. 3, March 16, 1993, pp. 6–9, in *FBIS-CHI*, March 22, 1993, pp. 15–18.

Xu Xin, *Changing Chinese Security Perceptions,* paper presented at the North Pacific Cooperative Security Dialogue Workshop on Changing National Military Security Perceptions, Yokohama, Japan, August 28–29, 1992.

Yahuda, Michael, "The Foreign Relations of Greater China," *China Quarterly,* No. 136, December 1993, pp. 687–710.

Yan Shi (pseudonym), "Provinces Hold Key to Reform," *Far Eastern Economic Review,* December 27, 1990, p. 16.

Yang, Richard H. (ed.), *China's Military: The PLA in 1992/1993* (Chinese Council of Advanced Policy Studies, Taipei, Taiwan), Westview Press, Boulder, Colorado, 1993.

Yeung, Yue-man, and Xu-wei Hu (eds.), *China's Coastal Cities: Catalysts for Modernization,* University of Hawaii Press, Honolulu, 1992.

Yü Yü-lin, "The PLA's Political Role After the CCP's Thirteenth National Congress: Continuity and Change," *Issues and Studies,* Vol. 24, No. 9, September 1988, pp. 11–35.

Yukawa, Kazuo, "Economic Cooperation Between Guangdong and Inland Areas," *JETRO China Newsletter,* No. 100, September–October, 1992, pp. 9–16.

Zang Xiaowei, "Elite Formation and the Bureaucratic-Technocracy in Post-Mao China," *Studies in Comparative Communism,* Vol. 24, No. 1, March 1991, pp. 114–123.

Zang Xiaowei, "Provincial Elite in Post-Mao China," *Asian Survey,* Vol. 31, No. 6, June 1991, pp. 512–525.

Zang Xiaowei, "The Fourteenth Central Committee of the CCP: Technocracy or Political Technocracy?" *Asian Survey,* Vol. 33, No. 8, August 1993, pp. 787–803.

Zhao Suisheng, "Beijing's Perception of the International System and Foreign Policy Adjustment in the Post–Cold War World," *Journal of Northeast Asian Studies,* Fall 1992, pp. 70–83.

Zhao Suisheng, "Deng Xiaoping's Southern Tour: Elite Politics in Post-Tiananmen China," *Asian Survey*, Vol. 33, No. 8, August 1993, pp. 739–756.

Zuckerman, Laurence, "Defying Gravity," *Asian Wall Street Journal*, October 18, 1993, pp. S-2, S-27.